A–Z
OF
KEW AND BRENTFORD
PLACES - PEOPLE - HISTORY

Andy Bull

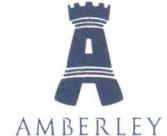

Acknowledgements

Grateful thanks are extended to all those authors quoted in this book, and to the photographers who have made their work available under Creative Commons.

Every attempt has been made to seek permission for copyright material used. However, if we have inadvertently used copyright material without permission/acknowledgement we apologise and will make the necessary correction at the first opportunity.

First published 2025

Amberley Publishing
The Hill, Stroud, Gloucestershire, GL5 4EP
www.amberley-books.com

Copyright © Andy Bull, 2025

The right of Andy Bull to be identified as the Author of this work has been asserted in accordance with the Copyrights, Designs and Patents Act 1988.

ISBN 978 1 3981 1715 0 (print)
ISBN 978 1 3981 1716 7 (ebook)

All rights reserved. No part of this book may be reprinted or reproduced or utilised in any form or by any electronic, mechanical or other means, now known or hereafter invented, including photocopying and recording, or in any information storage or retrieval system, without the permission in writing from the Publishers.

British Library Cataloguing in Publication Data.
A catalogue record for this book is available from the British Library.

Typesetting by SJmagic DESIGN SERVICES, India.
Printed in Great Britain.

Appointed GPSR EU Representative: Easy Access System Europe Oü, 16879218
Address: Mustamäe tee 50, 10621, Tallinn, Estonia
Contact Details: gpsr.requests@easproject.com, +358 40 500 3575

Contents

Introduction	5	HMS *Bounty*	37
		Hooker, Sir William	37
Adams, John Quincy	6		
Anglo-Saxon Era	7	Impressionism	39
Astronaut	8	Industry	39
Banks, Sir Joseph	10	Jam	42
Boston Manor House	11	Jewish Settlement	43
Brentford FC	12		
Brentford Nylons	14	Kangaroos	45
Brompton Bicycles	15	Kew	45
		Kew Bridge	46
Caesar	16	Kew's First Gardeners	47
Canal and Docks	16	Kew Green	47
Caxton Name Plate Manufacturing Company	18		
Chrysler and Dodge	18	Lucozade Sign	50
Concorde's Final Journey	19		
		Magistrates' Court, Brentford	52
Dickens, Charles	21	Maids of Honour	53
Dung	22	Martyrs	54
Dutch House, The	23	Merlin's Cave	54
		Monument, The	55
Elephants	24	Musical Museum, The	57
Fifty Pubs of Brentford	25	National Archives	59
Firestone Factory	26		
Fishing	28	Observatory, Kew	61
Fords and Ferries	29	Oliver's Ait	62
Fountain	30		
		Palm House, The	63
Gas	31	*People Just Do Nothing*	64
George III	31	Pocahontas	66
Great Pagoda, The	33	Pope, Alexander	67
Grey, Lady Jane	34		
Griffin	35	Queen Elizabeth I	68

Rankin, Robert	69	Underwood and Son	86
Rayon	70		
Red Barn Murder, The	71	V1 and V2 Flying Bombs	88
Regeneration	72		
		Watermans Arts Centre	89
Shakespeare, William	74	Wholesale Fruit and	
Smith's Crisps	76	Vegetable Market, Brentford	90
St Anne's Church	78		
St Lawrence's Church	79	X Bee Inspired	92
Steam Museum	80		
Suffragettes	81	York Mineral Water Company	93
Syon House	81		
		Zoffany, Johann	94
Temperate House	83		
Three Brentfords	83	Bibliography	96
Two Kings of Brentford	85		

Introduction

Kew and Brentford are not so much separated by the River Thames as connected through it. The existence from the earliest times of a ford here – the lowest point on the tidal stretch of the great river that could easily be crossed on foot – meant many travellers have passed through down the centuries.

Perhaps the most famous was Julius Caesar, who is believed to have crossed from what is now Kew to Brentford during his invasion of Britain in 54 BC, and did battle with the native Cassivellaunus here.

However, the two towns, connected by Kew Bridge, are very different from each other. Kew is a leafy middle-class suburb universally known for its Royal Botanic Gardens, often called, simply, Kew Gardens. Brentford has historically been a far grittier place, a mix of docks and factories. In the 1970s it briefly entered the national consciousness thanks to Brentford Nylons, a purveyor of static-charged sheets and polycotton nighties.

All that has changed in recent years. Since they joined the Premier League in 2021, Brentford is best known for its very successful football team. The area has also seen enormous rejuvenation, with riverside apartments steadily replacing the wharfs and warehouses.

With both Brentford and Kew there is much more to be revealed, and many more stories to tell, about these two mismatched towns.

The River Thames, with Kew to the right, Brentford to the left. (Andy Scott under Creative Commons)

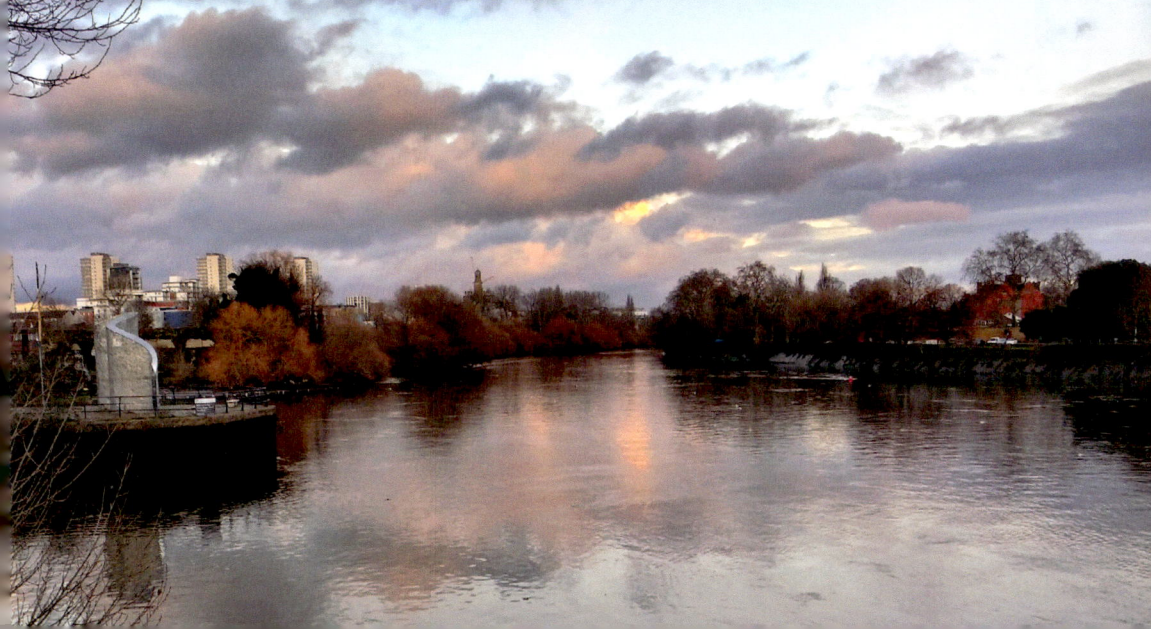

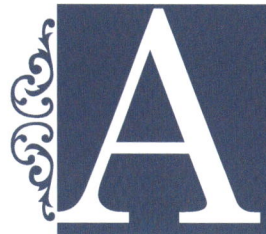

Adams, John Quincy

The man who would become the United States of America's sixth president lived in Brentford while ambassador to the UK. He had negotiated the peace treaty between Britain and America to end the war of 1812, fought between the US and Great Britain because of differences over territorial expansion and the treatment of indigenous peoples.

John Quincy Adams (1767–84), whose father John Adams had been America's second president, lived with his family in Little Boston House, which stood at the junction of

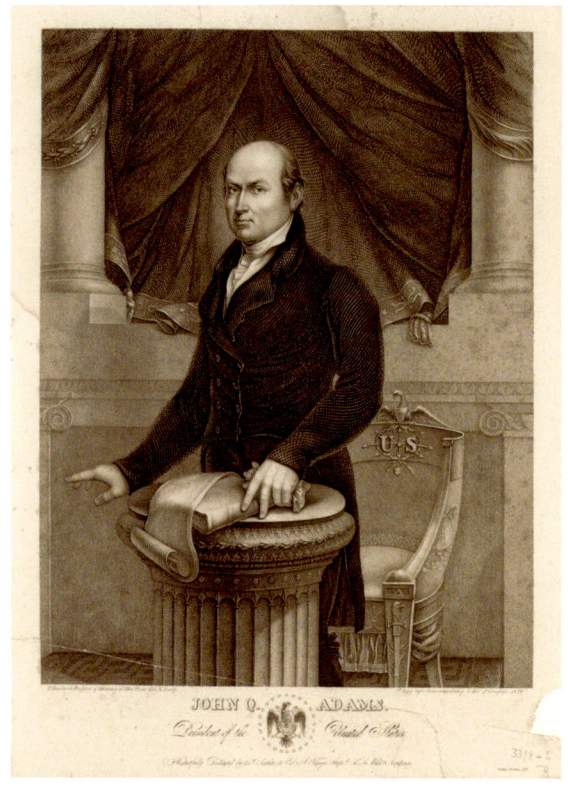

John Quincy Adams: from Brentford to the American presidency. (Library of Congress)

Windmill Road and The Ride, from 1815 to 1817. Adams kept a detailed diary, in which he said the house was 'as neat and elegant and fitted up with all that minute attention to comfort which is characteristic of English domestic life'.

He recorded many aspects of daily life in Brentford, including an account of visiting Brentford Fair in September 1815:

> We saw at one of the shows a double-jointed ox, between two and three feet high, a sheep with five legs, an armadillo, a jackall and a baboon. We also stopped and saw general people looking through a magic lanthorn, the showman of which announced that it was a view of the burning of the city of Washington, by General Ross ...
>
> While we were listening to him in the crowd I felt a hand making a plunge at my coat pocket, and was in time to prevent its getting in – this was another kind of British hostility from which it was expedient to remove, and we returned home. The fair is confined within the limits of the Market Square and is frequented only by children and the rabble.

Little Boston House, a substantial home with stables, dairy, a coach house and gardens, was owned by the Clitherow family who lived at Boston Manor. It was demolished in the 1820s. John Quincy Adams was president from 1920 to 1929.

Anglo-Saxon Era

The earliest written record referring to the area known today as Middlesex comes in 704, when it was known as Middelseaxe. The first use of the name Brentford comes a year later when it is mentioned, as Breguntford, in a treaty.

Breguntford lay at a significant place, between the kingdoms of the West and East Saxons – Wessex and Essex. For that reason it was used as the location for a series of meetings at which disputes between the two Saxon tribes could be resolved.

In 705 Breguntford was the location for a meeting to resolve a dispute over West Saxon exiles now living in the other kingdom. It is referred to in a letter from the Bishop of London, Waldhere, who was writing to Brihtwald, Archbishop of Canterbury. Waldhere writes that the West Saxon King, Ine, had agreed to submit the matter to the bishops of both kingdoms for resolution. Both kings would attend, along with nobles and clergy.

Three years later, Breguntford hosted a meeting of the Council of Offa, King of Mercia, which by then included the territory of the East Saxons. Offa attended along with his queen. The following year, at the Synod of Breguntford, a dispute was settled between Offa and the Bishop of Worcester.

These kings, nobles and bishops may have met at The Hamm, off the High Street – 'ham' being a Saxon name meaning township or homestead of the chieftain. However, excavations in 1966 failed to turn up any evidence of such a place.

A–Z of Kew and Brentford

Astronaut

When Helen Sharman responded to a radio advertisement that began: 'Astronaut wanted. No experience necessary', she was taking the first step on a remarkable journey. It led to her becoming the first Briton to reach outer space. Helen, who lives in Kew, also has the distinction of being the first Western European woman in space, and the first woman aboard the Mir space station.

She made the trip, in 1991, having beaten 13,000 other applicants and being accepted onto Project Juno, a joint venture between Russia and the UK designed to ease relations between the two countries following the end of the Cold War.

Helen, who was born in 1963 and who has a hugely distinguished career as a chemist, was selected in a process that gave weight to scientific, educational and aerospace

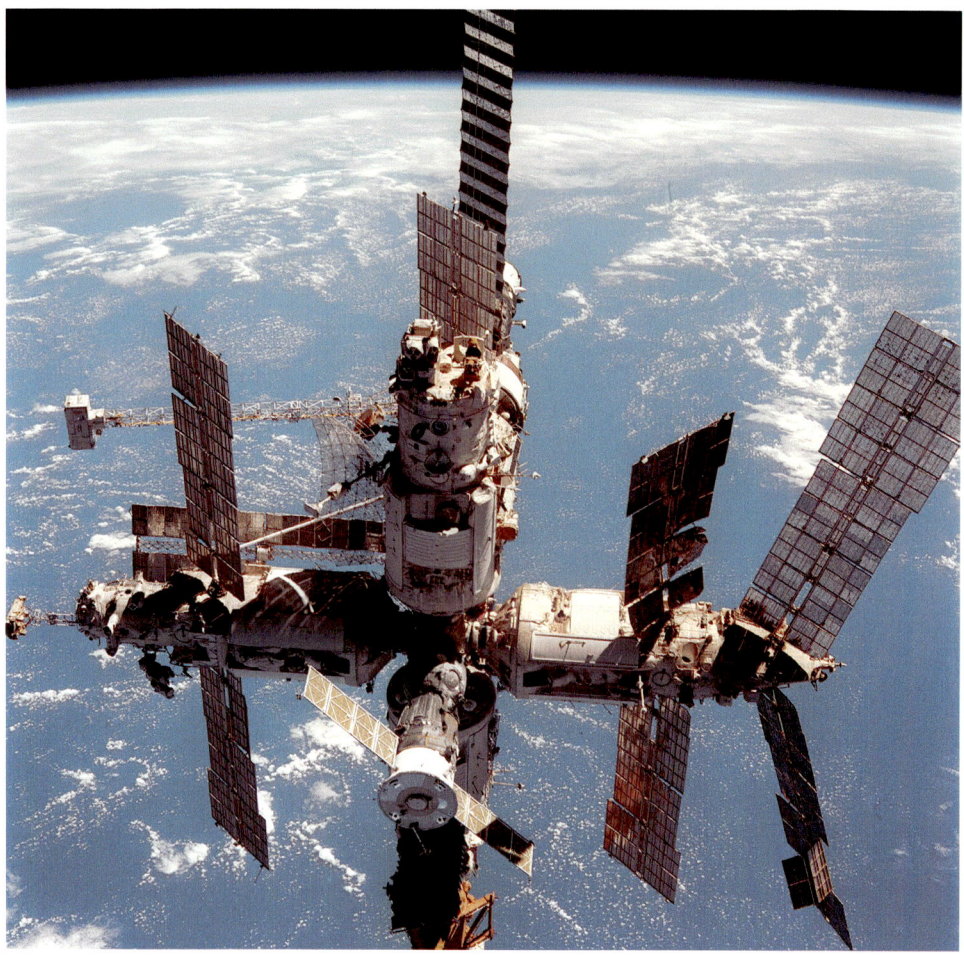

Above and opposite: Helen Sharman, the first woman on the Mir space station. (NASA/Anne-Katrin Purkiss under Creative Commons)

A

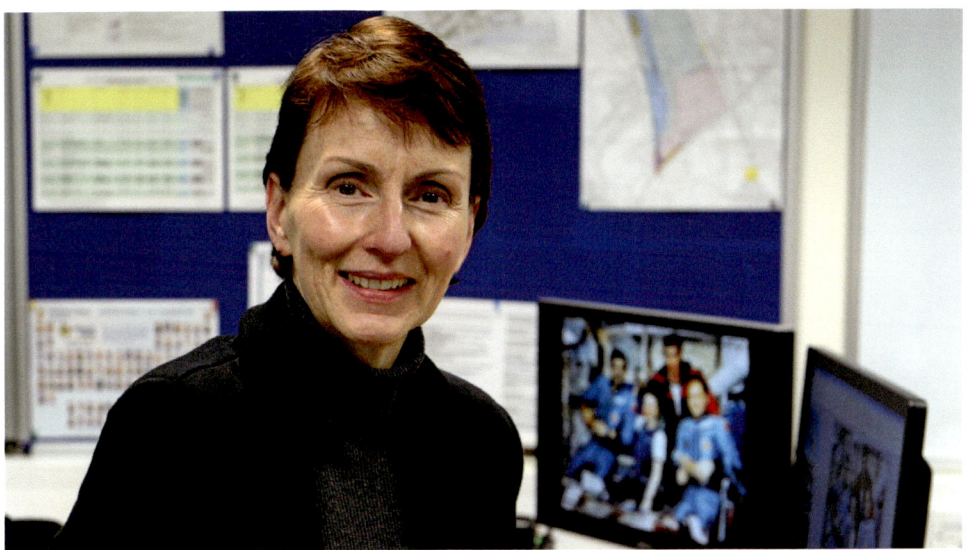

backgrounds, plus an ability to learn Russian. She spent eighteen months training in Russia, and said of the experience: 'It wasn't so much going to space as the training that appealed, living in Russia, learning the language, doing advanced mechanics. It was a way out of the rat race.'

She flew to Mir aboard the Soyuz TM-12 spacecraft and spent eight days on the station, where she conducted medical and agricultural experiments, photographed her homeland and took part in a radio broadcast with British schoolchildren. She carried a special space passport in case, on returning to Earth, she landed outside Russia.

When, during her training, it looked like the funding could not be raised to send her on the full mission, Helen was asked if she would settle for a short trip in which she would 'do nothing other than float about and make a few broadcasts back to Earth'. 'I said "No!" because I wanted that spaceflight to be useful and I would rather let someone else be that astronaut in the future if that would be more worthwhile.'

Her trip did not go entirely smoothly. The automatic docking system failed and the crew had to perform the manoeuvre manually. Helen later wrote on the kewtw9 website:

> My task was to operate a periscopic camera so the commander could see where he was going. If we missed the space station by a mile, we could have a second attempt at docking, but if we missed the docking port by a few centimetres, we could damage our spacecraft and the station sufficiently that we would all die.
>
> We knew that we relied on each other for our lives. Having docked safely and opened the hatch into the station, I still remember that amazing feeling of togetherness as I hugged the cosmonauts who had been on board for the six months before my launch. Nearly thirty years on, my crew and I are still friends.

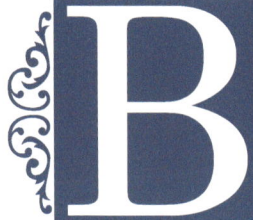

Banks, Sir Joseph

At the age of twenty-five, Joseph Banks persuaded Captain Cook to take him and five other keen botanists and scientists on his first great voyage of discovery in the *Endeavour*.

Banks and his team made collections at Rio de Janeiro, Tierra del Fuego, Tahiti, New Zealand and Australia. They returned with a huge collection of seeds and plants, along with shells, insects, bottled specimens and native implements.

On his return he advised George III and his wife Charlotte on the development of their botanic garden, today known as the Royal Botanic Gardens, or Kew Gardens. He established a great collection of exotic plants from all over the world.

Banks (1743–1820) spent fifty years living much of the time at Isleworth, and spending his own money sending young botanists around the world to gather

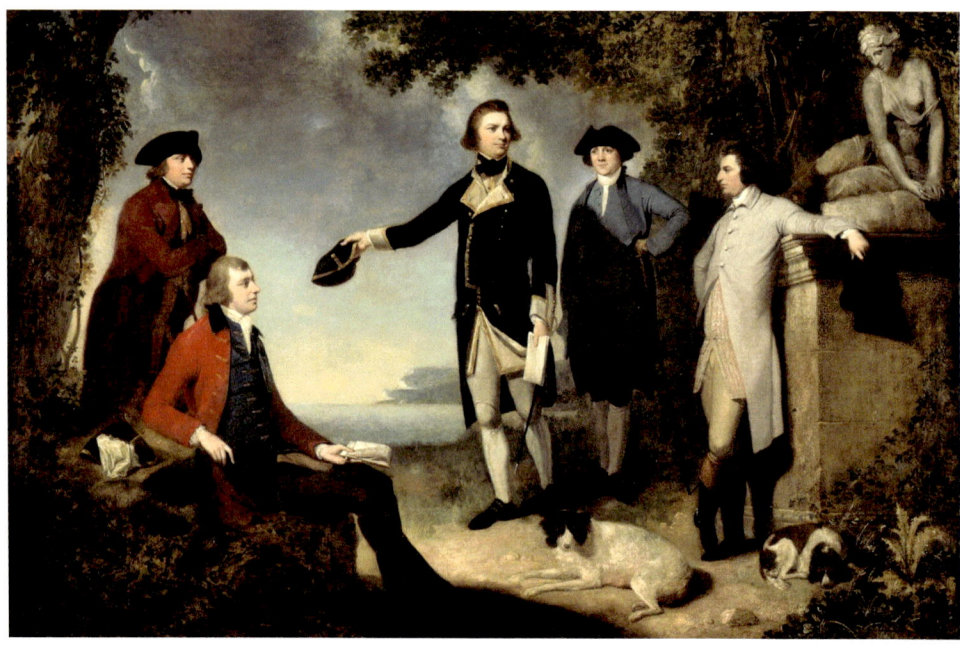

Sir Joseph Banks (second left) with Captain Cook (centre). (National Library of Australia)

B

promising plants. Thanks to his efforts, almost 7,000 exotic species were introduced, including hydrangeas and tree peonies.

Boston Manor House

Boston Manor House was at the heart of an estate that covered a swathe of modern-day Brentford, with lands running south from the present location of the Piccadilly line to the Thames, and bordered to the west by the River Brent and to the east by Boston Manor Road and Half Acre.

The present, recently extensively restored house dates from the early seventeenth century, but the estate is listed in the Domesday Book of 1086, and previous houses are mentioned in 1377 and 1584. Boston Manor has been owned down the centuries by a mix of wealthy merchants, a religious order, and the Crown.

It was seized from the religious order then in occupation by Henry VIII, in 1539, and later given by Elizabeth I to her favourite, Robert Dudley, Earl of Leicester, who immediately sold it to Sir Thomas Gresham, a rich merchant whose summer residence was at Osterley, a few miles to the north-west.

The present, three-storey, red-brick Jacobean manor house was built for Lady Mary Reade in 1622–3, and her initials and the completion date appear in the drawing room ceiling. This highly ornate ceiling is one of the real treasures in the house, and includes emblems depicting war and peace; the elements; the senses; time; and faith, hope and charity.

Lady Mary married into the Spencer family, of Althorp in Northamptonshire, in 1635. Sir Edward Spencer was an ancestor of Princess Diana, late first wife of

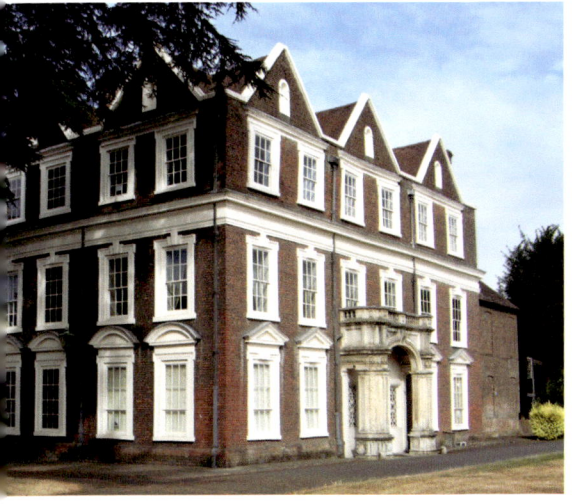 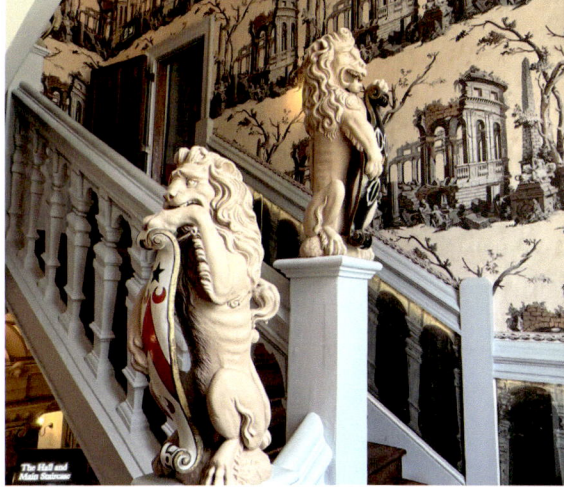

Above left and above right: Boston Manor House and its ornate interior. (Jim Linwood under Creative Commons, and courtesy London Borough of Hounslow)

Charles III. The couple were Royalists, and by some accounts hosted Charles I during the Battle of Brentford.

The Clitherow family were the next owners, the house and grounds remaining in their hands from 1670 until 1923, making numerous alterations and additions down the centuries. It took four years to sell the house, which by this time had become neglected and run-down. The contents, including hugely valuable works of art by Hogarth, Reubens and Van Dyke, were auctioned and the house, plus 20 acres of land, was bought by Brentford Urban District Council for the bargain price of £23,000 (£1.2 million today, according to the Bank of England's Inflation Calculator).

Some of the land was sold for housing and the rest landscaped to provide playing fields. The house has been home to a number of tenants since then. From 1940 to 1961 the ground floor became Boston Manor House Infants School, but extensive woodworm and dry rot forced the school to close.

After restoration, and a reopening ceremony conducted by Queen Elizabeth, the Queen Mother, the house became the headquarters of the National Institute of Houseworkers, which offered training to raise the skills of domestic workers (servants), enabling them to earn higher wages.

In 1972 the Over Forties Association for Women took on the lease. Its aim was to provide affordable homes for single women. Part of the house was converted into flats and bedsits and, in 1993, after the association had been renamed Housing for Women, seven more flats were built in the old stable block.

In the 1990s, the dining room and library, in addition to the State Drawing Room, which had always been open to the public, were restored and opened for visitors. Two Clitherow family portraits sold at the 1922 auction were bought and returned to the house.

Major work was again required in the present century, and the house was closed from 2018 until 2023 while a full restoration was undertaken, funded by the National Lottery Heritage Fund and other heritage organisations.

Brentford FC

Brentford Football Club has achieved national fame since being promoted to the Premier League in 2021, yet the town very nearly never got a football club at all.

On 10 October 1889 the members of Brentford Rowing Club had gathered at the Cambridge Hotel, which stood close to Kew Bridge, to decide what winter sport the rowers might pursue. Both rugby and football were on the table. Football won by a single vote.

Football had only become an organised sport with clear rules in 1871, when the Football Association was formed. In those early days, players were amateurs and grounds open fields.

Brentford's first ground was such a field, at the junction of Boston Manor Road and Windmill Road, and its clubhouse and changing rooms a few streets away at the Griffin pub in Brook Road. However, this ground was only available for three seasons,

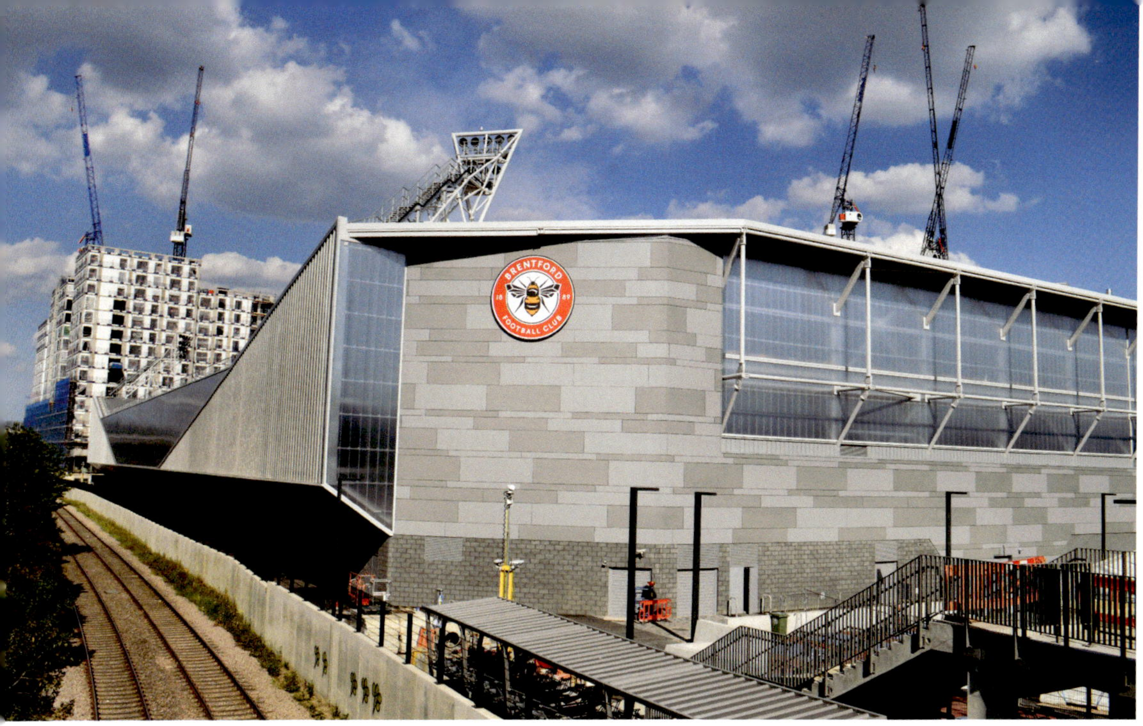

Above and right: Brentford FC's new G-Tech Community Stadium (Andy Scott under Creative Commons) and the Bees' Superstore.

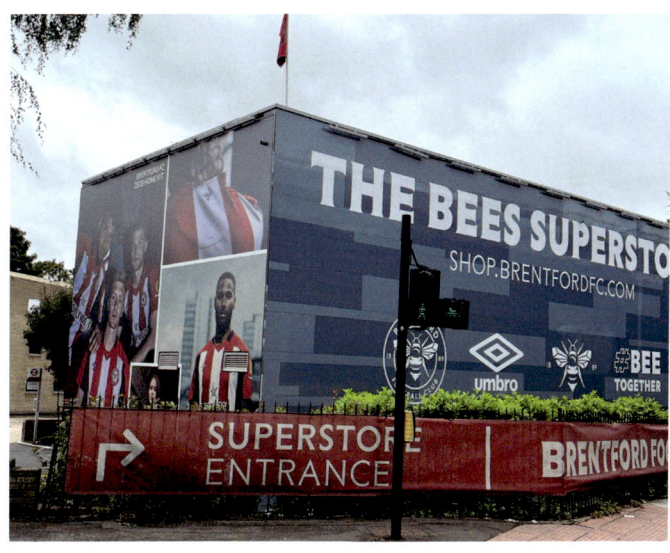

and the club was without a permanent home for several years. It rented fields across a wide area, some of them not in Brentford at all: Little Ealing, Shotters Field in Windmill Road, Cross Road in South Ealing and, from 1900 to 1904, shared a ground with Boston Park Cricket Club in York Road.

The club turned professional in 1900 and, in 1904, leased Griffin Park, which would become its permanent ground until 2021. In that year it moved to the new, purpose-built G-Tech Community Stadium close to Kew Bridge in Lionel Road South. Griffin Park was built on an orchard belonging to the Fuller Smith and Turner Brewery and, fortuitously, the Griffin pub stood at one corner.

Prior to its present Premier League status, the club's glory days were in the 1930s. In 1932–3 it won the Third Division (South) Championship and then, two years later, became Second Division champions. On 5 September 1935 Brentford made their home debut in what was then the top division, beating Blackburn Rovers 2-0 before a 30,000-strong crowd. Their fifth-place finish made them the highest-placed London club in the league.

The Second World War saw an end to the normal fixture list, but in 1942 Brentford won the London War Cup at Wembley Stadium. Post-war, Brentford's fortunes faded and they had dropped to the Fourth Division by 1962. In 1967, fans fought off a proposed merger with Queens Park Rangers.

The renaissance began in 2009 when the club were champions of League Two, and continued in 2014 when they were promoted from League One to the Championship. They were twice the nearly-men, in 2015 and 2020, where they lost out to promotion rivals during the play-offs.

Brentford Nylons

The firm synonymous with static-charged bri-nylon sheets and lurid adverts by the DJ Alan Freeman really established the town in the public consciousness in the 1970s.

The commercials typically showed Freeman pulling up in his Triumph Stag convertible alongside the factory, built on Brentford's Golden Mile, followed by a succession of models in nylon nighties, on beds made up with nylon or polycotton blankets and sheets. At its height, the company had ninety stores around the country

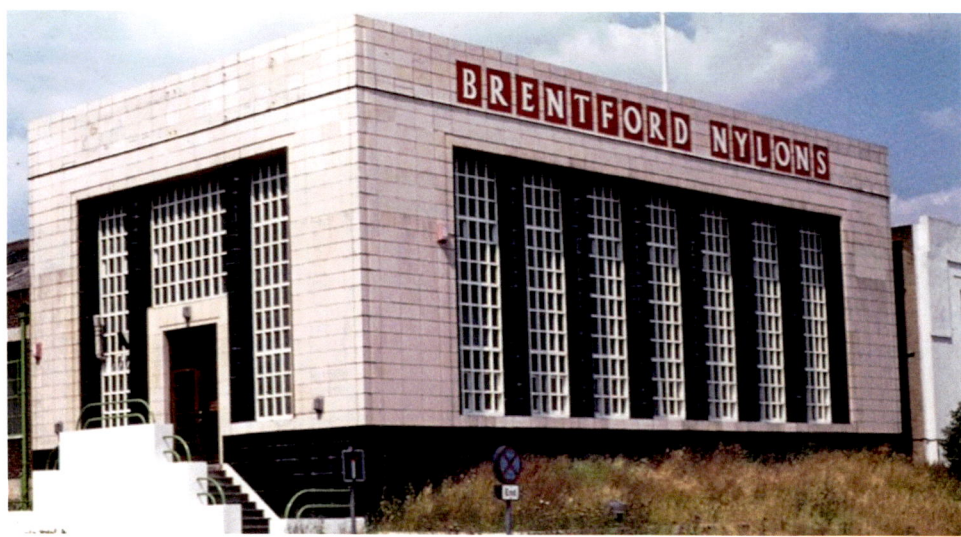

Above and opposite: Brentford Nylons and Brompton Bicycles were both once based in Brentford. (Peter Young and Kuttuurinanavigattori under Creative Commons)

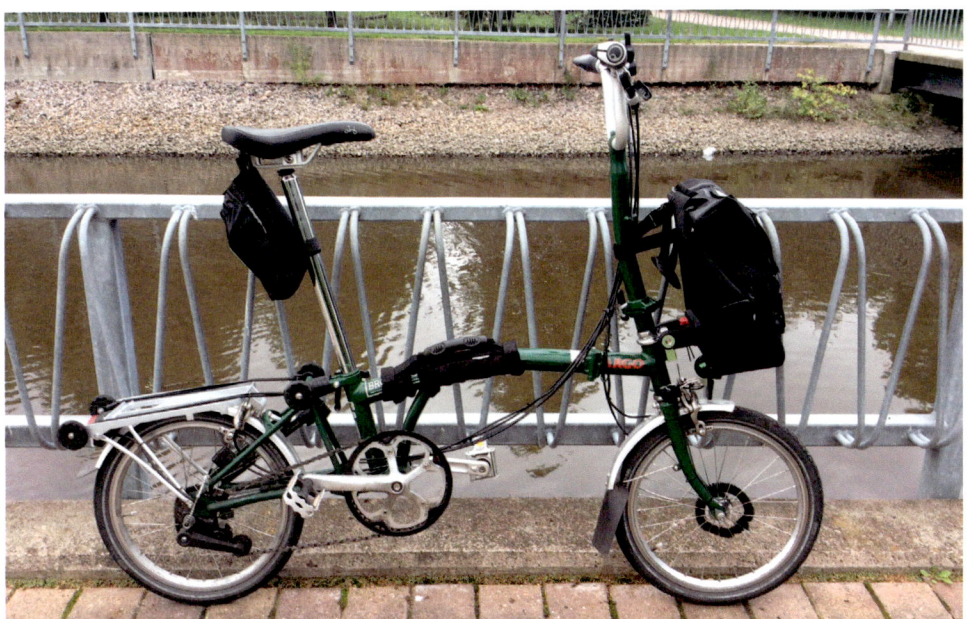

and a thousand employees. The firm had been founded by Harry Pambakian, an immigrant from Armenia.

Brentford Nylons' decline was precipitous. It went bust in 1976 and was bought out of receivership by the mining and textiles conglomerate Lonrho.

As Nigel Cope wrote in *The Independent*:

> The stores enjoyed their heyday in the 1970s when nylon sheets were popular, but soon lost favour in the more design-conscious 1980s. The name was later changed simply to Brentfords, but the business could never shrug off its downmarket image. The ninety stores made a loss of £2.3m [in 1995].

The company was sold that year to Roseby's, a Rotherham-based curtain and household goods retailer, which dropped the name Brentfords and merged the remaining shops into its own chain. Michael Rosenblatt, chief executive of Roseby's, said: 'Our research showed that the stores' main weak point was the name. People would sooner be seen with a plain white carrier than a Brentfords bag.'

Brompton Bicycles

Brompton folding bicycles were manufactured in a Brentford railway arch for thirty years, before the company moved a couple of miles north to Greenford, there becoming the largest UK cycle manufacturer.

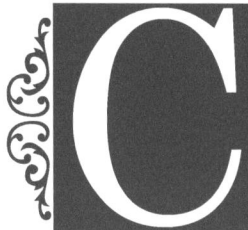

Caesar

Perhaps the most famous visitor to what are now Kew and Brentford was Julius Caesar, who is believed to have crossed from the site of the former to the latter during his invasion of Britain in 54 BC. Here he did battle with the native Cassivellaunus.

Written history for both towns begins at this point, for Caesar recorded his exploits in his book *Gallic Wars*. There he says he discovered that the River Thames was fordable at one point only, 75 miles upriver from the sea. He also recorded the existence of a defensive network of sharpened oak stakes, driven into the riverbed on both the Kew and Brentford banks. Many such stakes were found when Brentford Dock was constructed in the nineteenth century.

Canal and Docks

When, in 1793, George III gave his assent to an Act of Parliament for the excavation of a canal from the Thames at Brentford to Braunston in Northamptonshire, he was allowing the creation of the M1 of its day.

At a time when canals offered the most efficient way to transport heavy goods, the new route cut the journey time from London to the Midlands and made Brentford a hugely important transport hub: a convenient point at which cargoes brought from around the world to London Docks could be shipped upriver and, from here, distributed around the land. It also gave an ideal route for exports from the industrial heartland of the Midlands.

The first 12-mile section of the Grand Junction Canal, from Brentford to Uxbridge, was opened in 1794. In 1929 this canal was combined with a network of other routes to form the Grand Union Canal, which built a depot at Brentford where cargo could be transferred from river-vessel to narrowboat.

The dock was on the island between the canal and the River Brent, an area now developed as a gated community named The Island. The Grand Union was nationalised in 1948, and commercial traffic on the canal had ceased almost completely by the 1980s.

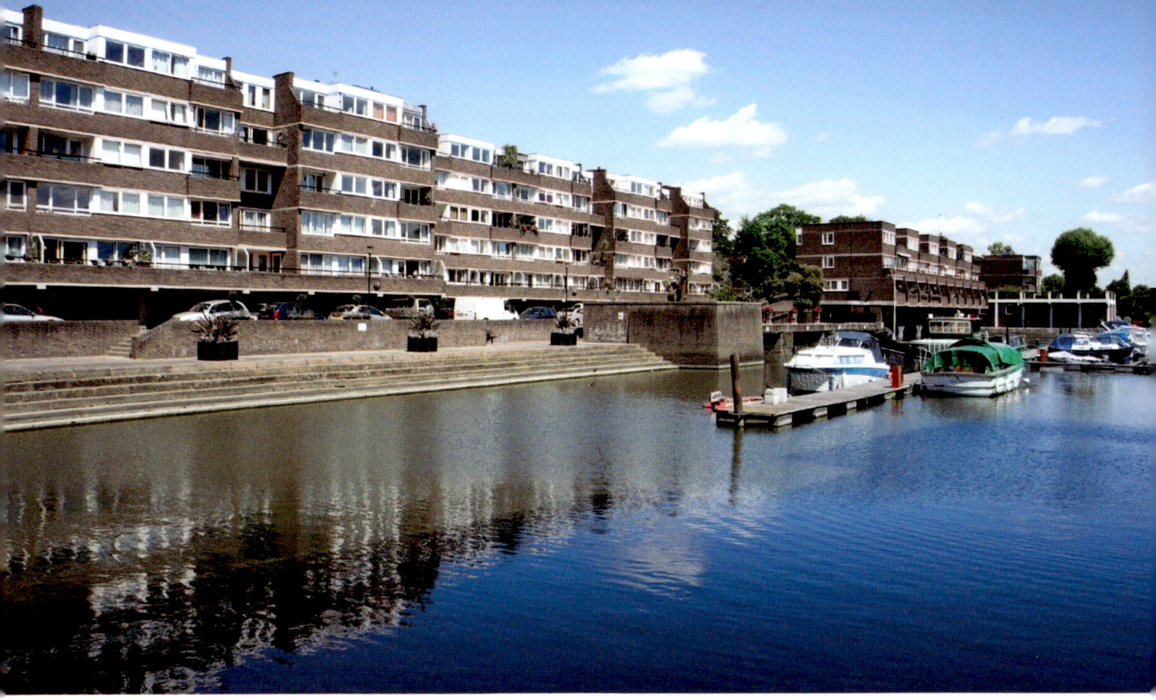

Above: The marina at Brentford Dock. (Maxwell Hamilton under Creative Commons)

Right: Brentford Lock on the Grand Union Canal. (Michael Coppins under Creative Commons)

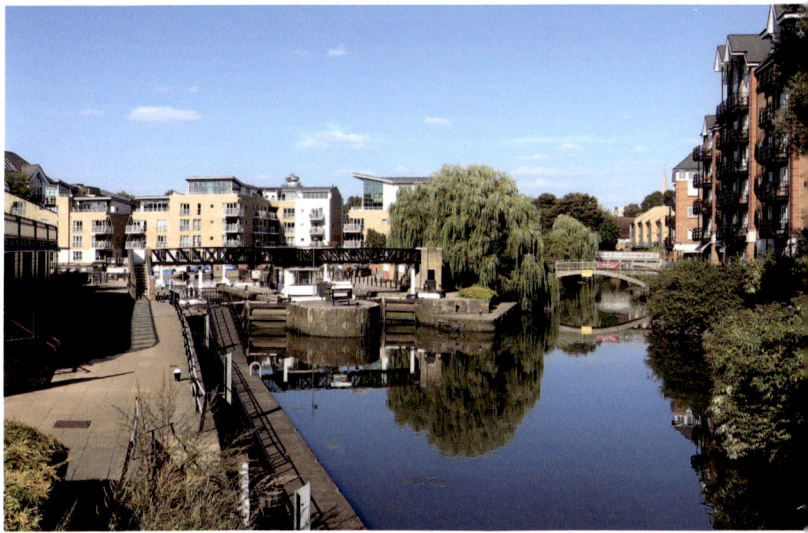

In 1859, the Great Western Railway ran a line to a purpose-built Brentford Dock, designed by Isambard Kingdom Brunel. Here, goods for export could be transferred from rail to barge, for shipment down-Thames to the London Docks, where they could be loaded onto ocean-going ships. Imports did the trip in reverse.

The Brentford branch line linked up with the main line between Paddington and the West Country, and until the 1940s carried passengers as well as goods.

The progressive closure of the London Docks during the latter half of the twentieth century rendered the facility redundant. The dock was closed in 1964 and was developed for housing and a marina by the Greater London Council in 1972.

Caxton Name Plate Manufacturing Company

Just South of Kew Bridge is the former factory where the Caxton Name Plate Manufacturing Company turned out millions of badges, and metal signs for railways, government departments and private companies.

Chrysler and Dodge

Kew once had its own car and lorry plant. Chrysler cars and Dodge trucks were produced where Kew Retail Park is now, on Mortlake Road.

Chrysler was an American company and opened the plant here in the 1920s to beat UK import restrictions. Parts were shipped in kit form from the US, and the cars assembled here. To appeal to British motorists they were given names such as the Chrysler Kew and Wimbledon, plus the DeSoto Richmond and Kingston.

After the Second World War, Dodge, Chrysler's truck brand, produced the Kew lorry here. Its nickname, Parrot Nose, was due to the sculpted lines of its bonnet. Production ceased in 1967 when the firm moved to Dunstable.

Prior to Chrysler's arrival, aeroplanes were manufactured at the plant. From 1918, the Glendower Aircraft company built the Airco DH.4s, a two-seater bomber, and

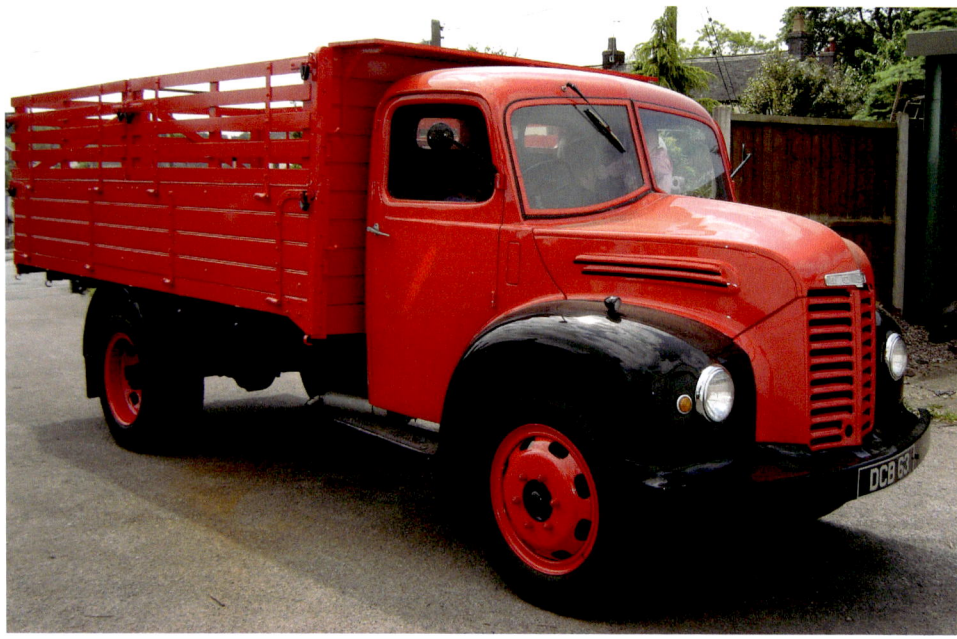

Dodge Kew, the parrot-nosed truck made in the town. (Mr Choppers under Creative Commons)

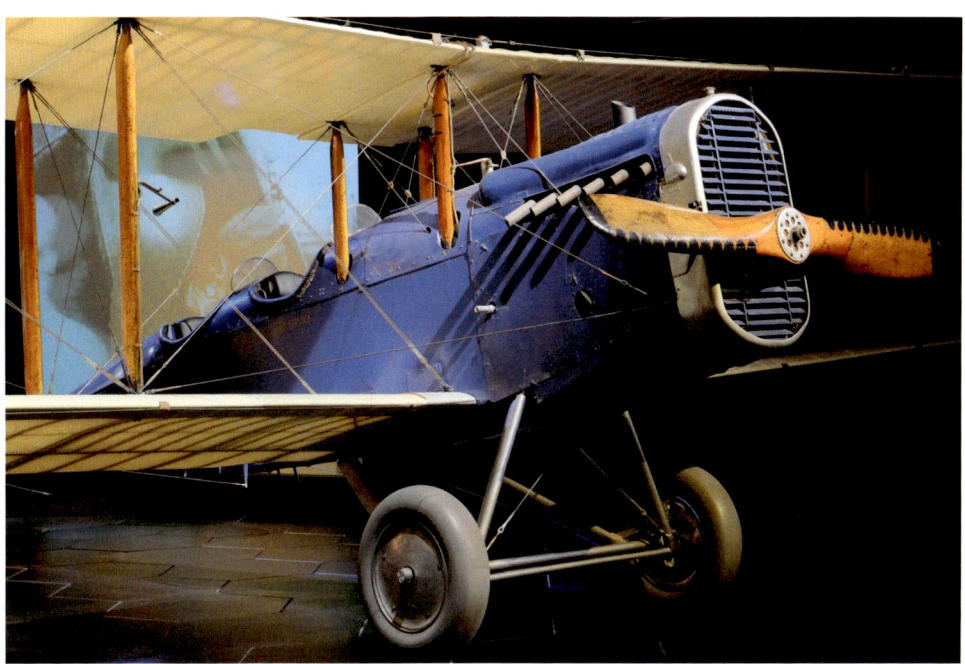

An Airco DH.4s, built during the First World War in Kew. (Pseudopanax under Creative Commons)

Sopwith Salamander, a single-seat ground attack aircraft. During the Second World War, the factory again switched to aircraft production, making fuselages for Handley Page Halifax bombers.

Concorde's Final Journey

Concorde, the supersonic aeroplane that scorched between London and New York in 2 hours and 53 minutes from 1973 to 1985, took its final journey through Brentford, at a considerably slower place and at zero feet above sea level.

The plane was taken by road from Heathrow, through Brentford and down to the Thames at Isleworth where, alongside the London Apprentice pub, it was loaded onto a barge to go down the Thames. It then transferred to a ship and went by sea up to Torness where it completed its journey overland to the National Museum of Flight at Edinburgh.

The journey through Brentford, on 8 April 2004, took place at night and residents were amazed to see the great plane being towed through the town. Jim Lawes later wrote on Facebook:

> It was a mind-blowing sight. I walked down Spur Road/Syon Lane with Concorde's wing above my head. It had been fitted with a roller-skate contraption and a wee cab which was steered by a skilled driver.

At Busch Corner more crowds gathered including a group of giggling girls, getting off a night bus, to be faced with this spectacle! Concorde had a rest at about 5.30 am in Park Road for a few hours. It was then guided to a spot by the London Apprentice, the Isleworth Dock in fact, to be loaded onto a waiting barge/transporter.

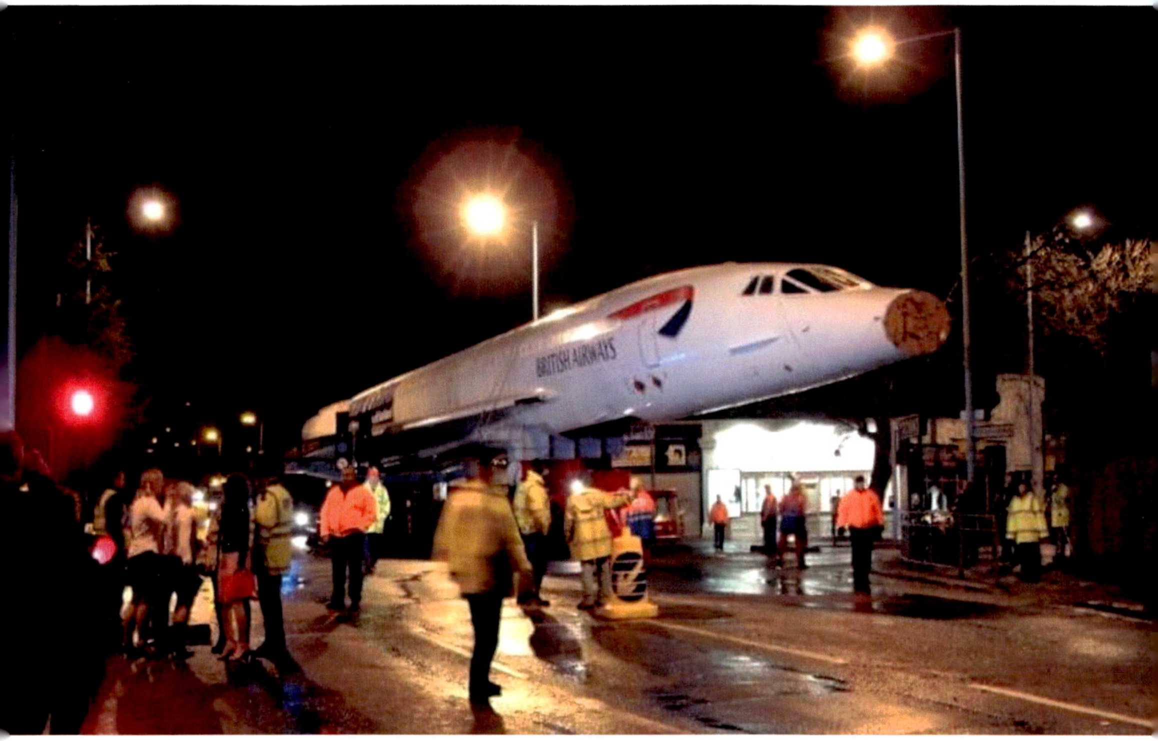

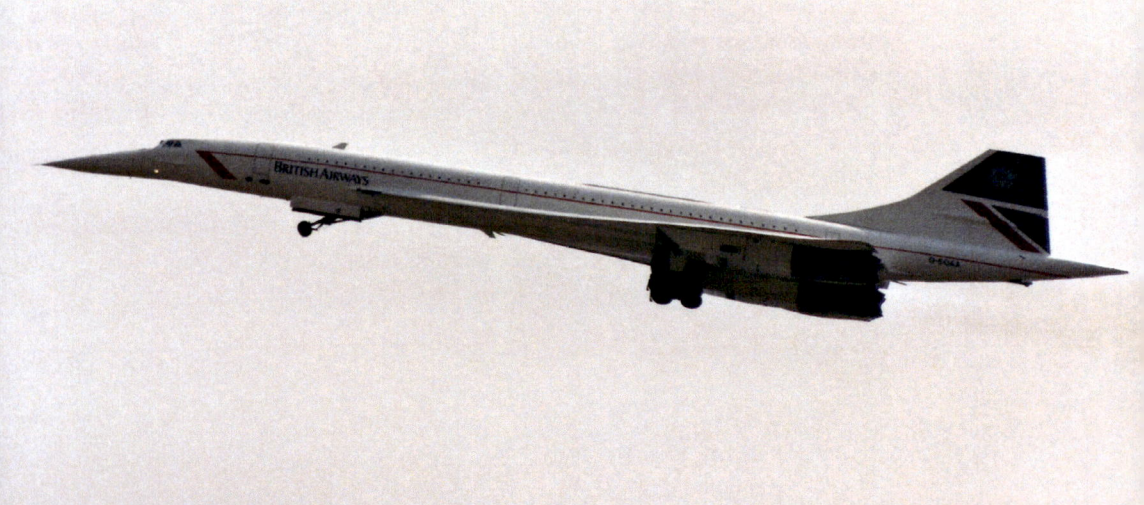

Above and below: Concorde during its final trip, via Brentford, and in flight. (Tony Hisgett and Kambui under Creative Commons)

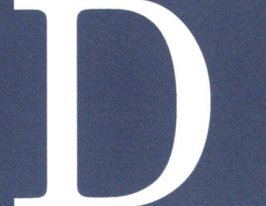

Dickens, Charles

In *Oliver Twist*, Bill Sikes and Oliver pass through Brentford on their way towards Shepperton to take part in a burglary. After passing along the High Street they stop at an Isleworth pub, the Coach and Horses at No. 183 London Road. Dickens writes:

> As they passed the different mile-stones, Oliver wondered, more and more, where his companion meant to take him. Kensington, Hammersmith, Chiswick, Kew Bridge,

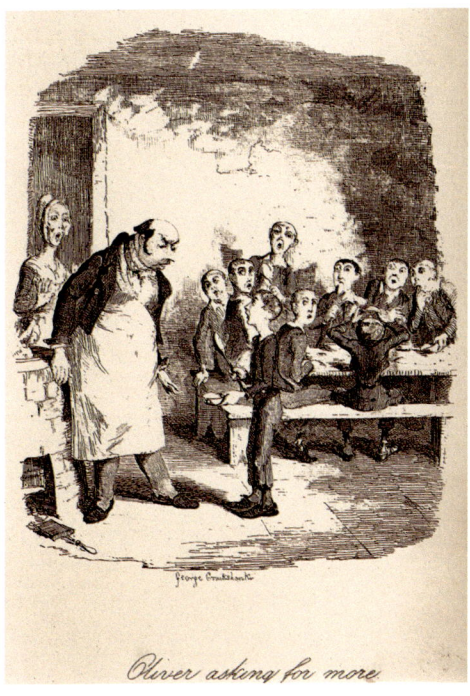
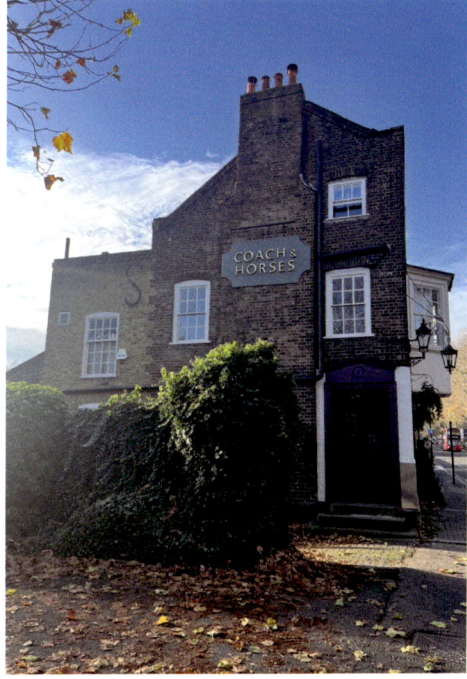

Above left: Oliver Twist, in an illustration by Cruikshank. (Wellcome Collection)

Above right: The Coach and Horses, which features in Charles Dickens's *Oliver Twist*.

Brentford, were all passed; and yet they went on as steadily as if they had only just begun their journey. At length, they came to a public-house called the Coach and Horses; a little way beyond which, another road appeared to run off. And here, the cart stopped.

The Coach and Horses dates from the seventeenth century and was a coaching inn. The bay window that projects from the first floor enabled travellers to see when their coach was approaching.

Oliver and Sikes had been given a lift this far in a cart. The novel continues:

Sikes dismounted with great precipitation, holding Oliver by the hand all the while; and lifting him down directly, bestowed a furious look upon him, and rapped the side-pocket with his fist, in a significant manner.

Their journey takes them on through Isleworth:

They turned round to the left, a short way past the public-house; and then, taking a right-hand road, walked on for a long time: passing many large gardens and gentlemen's houses on both sides of the way, and stopping for nothing but a little beer, until they reached a town. Here against the wall of a house, Oliver saw written up in pretty large letters, Hampton.

From there they continue to Shepperton, where the crime is to be committed.

Dung

The key ingredient in the growing of much-prized asparagus alongside the Thames at Kew in the nineteenth century was dung: human dung. As David Blomfield notes in *Kew Past*:

The soil beside the Thames was not particularly rich and the intensive farming of vegetables required the constant renewal of the soil. As a result, the vegetables were not so much grown in the soil of Kew as in layers of dung that the gardeners spread on top of it, the dung being brought nightly up-river from the City.

A market gardener called Mr Grayson was famous for his asparagus. 'In 1832 *The Gentleman's Magazine* reported that a bundle of asparagus that had 110 heads and weighed 29lbs had been presented to the Duchess of Bedford by Mr Grayson.'

Dutch House, The

The Dutch House, as Kew Palace was originally named, has the distinction of being the oldest house in Kew. It was rebuilt by Samuel Fortrey, a merchant, in 1631, in the Dutch style – hence the original name.

Fortrey was building on the undercroft of a great Tudor mansion, and the house he created has changed little since then. The entwined initials of Fortrey and his wife, Catherine La Fleur, can still be seen above the front door.

The house stands within Kew Gardens, but in the seventeenth century there were probably meadows behind the house, down to the River Thames, and gardens, orchards and woods before it.

In 1728 Queen Caroline, wife of George II, leased the house as a sort of overspill for their summer residence, Richmond Lodge. Their six children made the family too large for the lodge, and so Caroline had her three eldest daughters – Anne, Amelia and Caroline – billeted here. A generation later, it became a school house for Amelia's two eldest sons, George (the future George III) and Edward. George III's children were also housed here, making the Dutch House the nursery to three generations of royal children.

The Dutch House, now known as Kew Palace. (xlibber under Creative Commons)

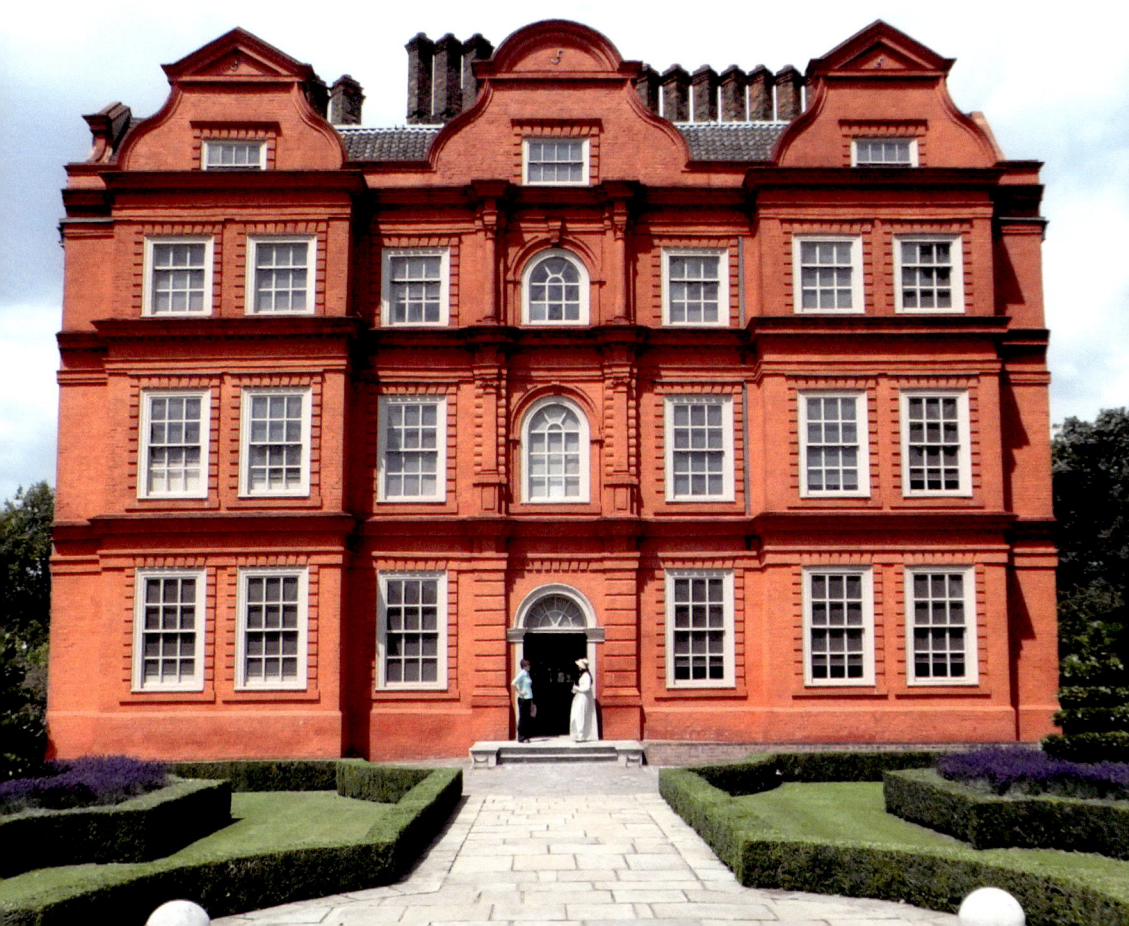

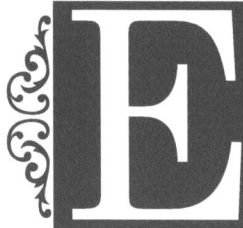

Elephants

During the Ice Age, elephants and a number of other now exotic creatures roamed Brentford and Kew. The fossilised remains of elephants, rhinos, hippos and lions were found in Brentford by a local archaeologist, William Kirby Trimmer. He published his findings in the *Philosophical Transactions of the Royal Society* in 1813. Trimmer's family were manufacturers of bricks and tiles, and the finds were discovered in clay pits being dug in Brentford. One elephant tusk uncovered measured a substantial 9 feet 3 inches. Trimmer found remains of both Asiatic and African elephants, plus numerous hippo bones and teeth.

F

Fifty Pubs of Brentford

There were once fifty pubs in Brentford, many of them crowded along the High Street. A poem exists, in a number of versions, that attempts to chronicle all of them.

'The Brentford Pubs Poem' names those encountered when walking westwards for just 1.25 miles from Kew Bridge along Kew Bridge Road, Brentford High Street and on along London Road to Brentford End.

However, as pubs opened and closed over the years, and some moved location or changed name, it has been a challenge to local pub historians to work out when the original version of the poem might have been written. The Brentford High Street Project lists five versions of the poem, and endorses the opinion of Vic Rosewarne that the pubs named all existed in 1883.

One version, according to *Brentford History*, was written by Alfred Pearce in 1948, when he was then aged seventy-four. In his day job Pearce was a foreman at Brentford Dock, by night he was an entertainer, and no doubt recited his poem is some of the many pubs he lists.

Pearce starts at the Star and Garter (converted into offices in 1984) on Kew Bridge Road, and proceeds west, ending up at the Coach and Horses. His version of the poem begins:

> When I was knighted with a STAR AND GARTER I was pushed into an EXPRESS
> On my way to OXFORD AND CAMBRIDGE I smashed into a PLOUGH
> And stood aside by the WAGGON AND HORSES a little beyond a JOLLY TAR
> With a LAMB by his side receiving a SALUTATION

Brentford was famous for its pubs and, from Roman times, travellers taking the main road to the west would stop here for refreshment. The first public house is recorded in the fourteenth century, and in 1888 the *County of Middlesex Independent Almanack and Directory* listed over sixty, suggesting the poets might have missed one or two.

By the start of this century the number had dropped to around twenty-five and today under twenty. The oldest pub is probably The Weir, formerly the White Horse, in Market Place. It was first mentioned in 1603.

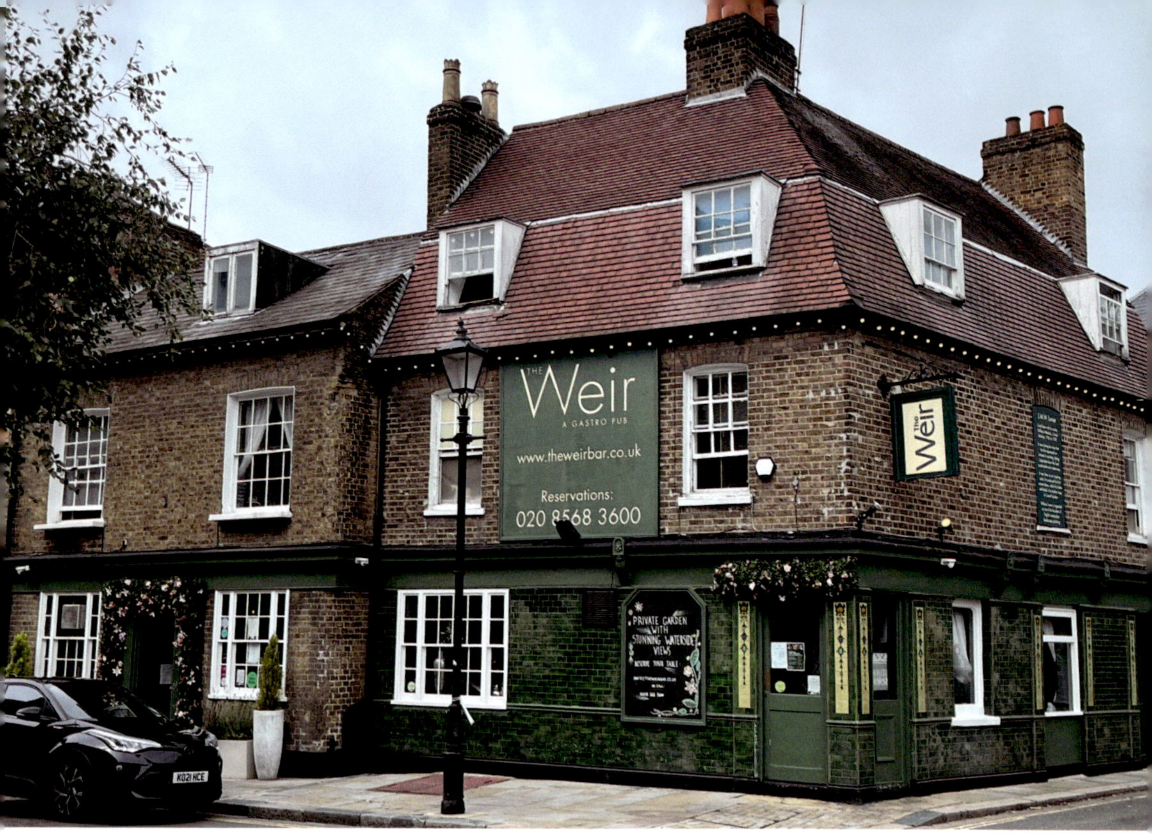

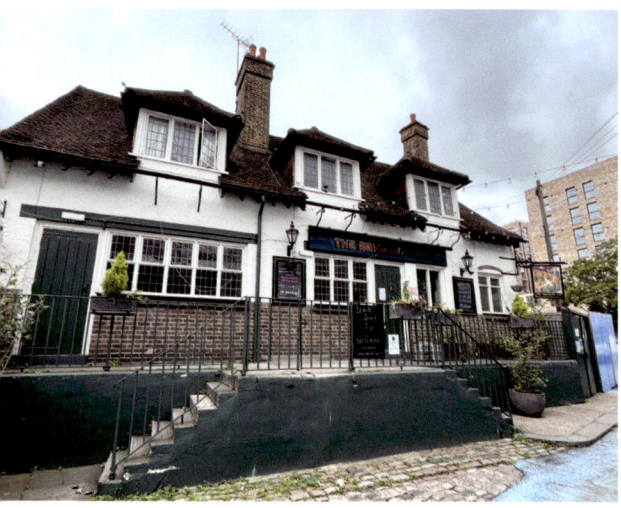

Above and left: The Weir, formerly the White Horse, and The Brewery Tap.

Firestone Factory

The elegant art deco Firestone Factory was a landmark on the Great West Road for fifty years, but it owed its existence to a rise in import duties on tyres. To avoid adding the 33.3 per cent tax to its products, the American Firestone Tyre and Rubber Company built a plant in Brentford in 1928.

F

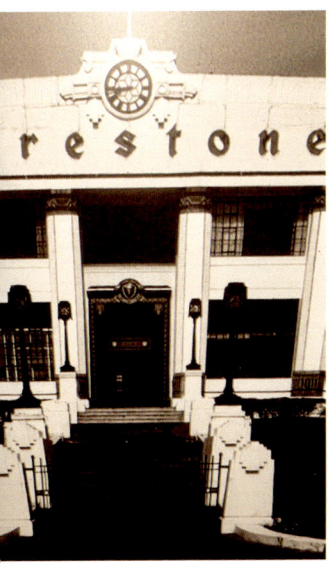
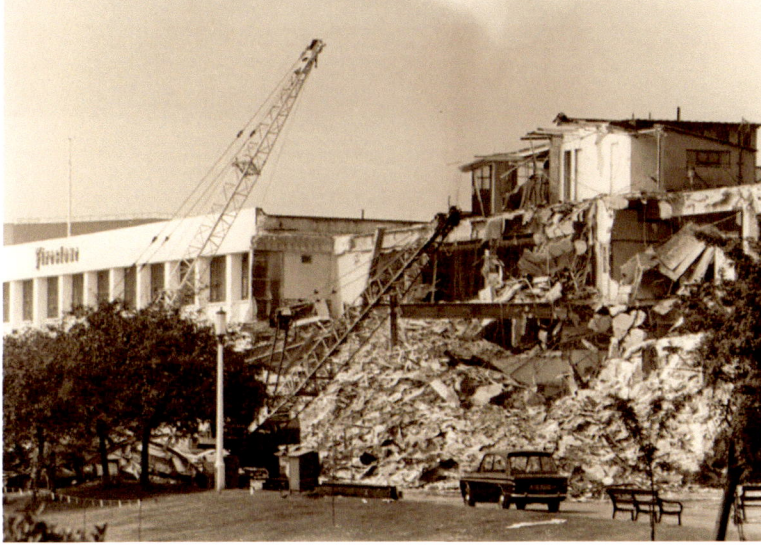
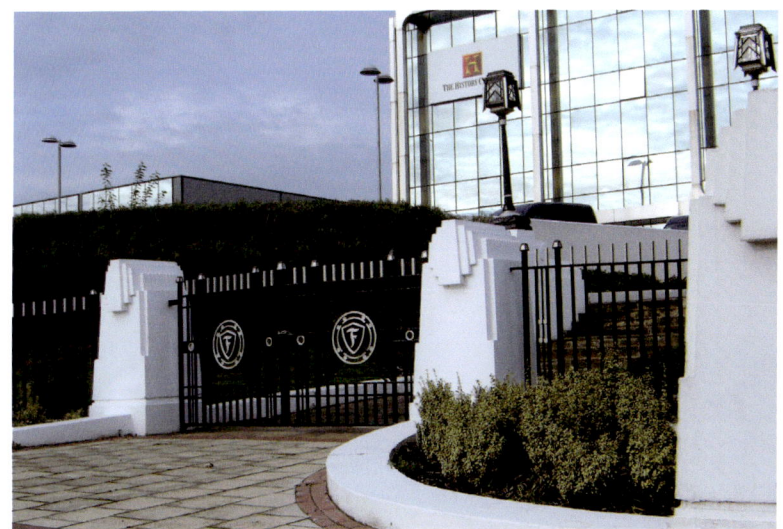

Above left, above right and right: The Firestone Factory, its destruction, and surviving gateway. (C. Wheatley and Kt0288 under Creative Commons)

The plant covered 26 acres and was only the second factory to be built alongside the then new trunk road to the West Country. It was designed by Wallis, Gilbert and Partners, a British architectural practice responsible for some of the finest art deco factories of the 1920s and 1930s. They also built the Hoover Building a few miles to the north on Western Avenue, Perivale. The Firestone Factory was the firm's greatest achievement. The *Modernism in Metroland* blog says of it:

The building was to act ... as an advert for the company and for what we would these days call its 'brand', looking to project speed, glamour and aspiration. The building was a mix of Classical allusions. In plan it was a Greek or Roman temple with its row of columns along the frontage, in detail it was Egyptian, with references to the gods Horus, Ra and Amun in its decoration.

Egyptian design was still popular six years after the discovery of the tomb of Tutankhamun by Howard Carter in 1922. By night the building was floodlit, producing a spectacular landmark along the Great West Road.

The Firestone Factory was not only an aesthetic delight, but a thoroughly practical building, designed for maximum efficiency.

Behind the main administration block facing the Great West Road was a single-storey production area and, behind that, a four-storey dispatch and storage building. Raw materials came into the storage area, were processed into tyres in the production block, before the finished tyres went back to the dispatch area.

There were lawns to the front of the building and, to the west, a sports ground for workers.

A combination of cheap imported tyres from Eastern Europe and controversy and problems at the parent company in America brought about its closure in 1979. Around 1,500 staff were made redundant. Gillian Clegg, in *Brentford Past*, writes:

> What happened next was an act of sheer vandalism. The building was purchased by a subsidiary of the Trafalgar House Property Group. When rumours began to circulate that its new owners were planning to demolish it, the Department of the Environment acted to schedule it as a listed building, but before the listing could be finalised, the building was gone. A demolition gang worked throughout the August Bank Holiday weekend of 1980 to reduce it to a pile of rubble. The original pillars, railings, gates and steps are all that remains.

Simon Jenkins of the Thirties Society, since renamed the Twentieth Century Society, commented: 'If ever there was a building from the inter-war period of British architecture that should have been retained, it was this one.'

The site is now occupied by Currys PC World, and industrial units in West Cross Way.

Fishing

Fishing was Kew and Brentford's largest industry for 300 years. Up until the 1800s, the Thames was a rich habitat for both fresh and saltwater fish, and supported a significant fishing industry. Yet inhabitants had been feeding on fish long before this period. Romano-British fishermen's huts stood on the riverbank at Brentford during the Roman occupation.

Down the centuries, the river's harvest was abundant. In the sixteenth century, according to the chronicler Holinshed, no river in Europe had more salmon than the Thames, which was also rich in trout, perch, bream, flounders and shrimps.

F

In 1769, Brentford was populated chiefly by poor fishermen and watermen, the water coming up to the doors of their riverside homes. However, as industry built up along the Thames in the 1800s, water quality began to fall, and there was a sharp decline in fish numbers. Things reached their nadir in 1957 when a Natural History Museum study found no fish at all between Kew and Gravesend.

There were two main fishing areas along this stretch of the river: the Westerly Ware and the Ware Ground, which was effectively the Easterly Ware. The Westerly stretched from a dock just to the east of Kew Bridge to Ferry Lane. The Easterly was upriver from there. In these stretches, Kew and Brentford fishermen would beach their boats, and dry and mend their nets.

The word 'ware' refers to the practice of creating weirs or 'wares' to catch fish. Wares were zig-zags of stakes driven into the riverbed supporting woven panels, or hurdles, in which fish became trapped, and from which they would be gathered in nets and brought ashore.

This history is referenced in the memorial garden near Kew Bridge called Westerly Ware, which honours the fallen in the First World War, and which also has tennis courts and a children's playground.

Fords and Ferries

The ford offering a key crossing point over the lower Thames between Kew and Brentford was probably around 200 yards upriver from the Brentford Ferry gate entrance to the Royal Botanic Gardens, running across to the area now covered by Brentford Dock. South from it, an ancient trackway led to Dover. As recently as the eighteenth century it was said, in Camden's *Britannica*, that the water here was just 3 feet deep at low tide.

There was also a ferry at roughly this point. Gillian Clegg, in *Brentford Past*, writes:

> A ferry between Brentford and Kew had been operating from time immemorial, probably from the bottom of Ferry lane. Residents of Old Brentford travelled free until 1536 when ferry keeper John Hale charged a halfpenny to take horsemen across and a farthing for pedestrians. By 1659 another ferry, for foot passengers only, had been started further east (near the present Kew Bridge).

This was operated by Henry Tunstall and his son Robert, and known as Powell's Ferry. It annoyed John Churchman, owner of the Kew Ferry, by undercutting his rates. Kew Ferry became known as the Royal Ferry when the Hanoverian kings made their home at Kew and Richmond. Clegg writes:

> Ferry receipt books show it was much used by royalty. In five days in August 1736, Frederick, Prince of Wales, son of George II, paid £2 2s 10d to transport 116 horses across the river, also 1s 6d for the conveyance of the prince's butcher's cart.

In 1759 the Tunstalls built the first Kew Bridge, and their ferry closed.

There was also a ford over the River Brent at a point where Commerce Road meets Brentford High Street. There are no prizes for deducing that this is how Brentford got its name. The word 'Brent' comes from the Celtic word *brigantia*, for holy or high water, and the first recorded use of the ford is in the eighth century.

Fountain

An ornate Victorian drinking fountain once stood in the centre of the road at the Brentford end of Kew Bridge. It was unveiled by Princess Mary, Duchess of Teck, in 1877, and formed the centre point of an informal market that grew up around it.

The grey granite fountain had two troughs for horses to drink from and, up four steps, four basins for human refreshment. At its centre an octagonal tower rose, topped with an elegant spire. It was shielded by cast-iron railings and illuminated by four gas lamps.

When the market moved to dedicated premises on Chiswick High Road in 1906, the fountain went with it. When that market was closed in 1974 it moved again, to Southall, and the Western International Market. In recent years it has suffered from neglect and vandalism and no longer holds water for man nor beast. In 2022 it was placed on Historic England's Heritage at Risk register. At the time of writing a new home was being sought for it, back in Brentford.

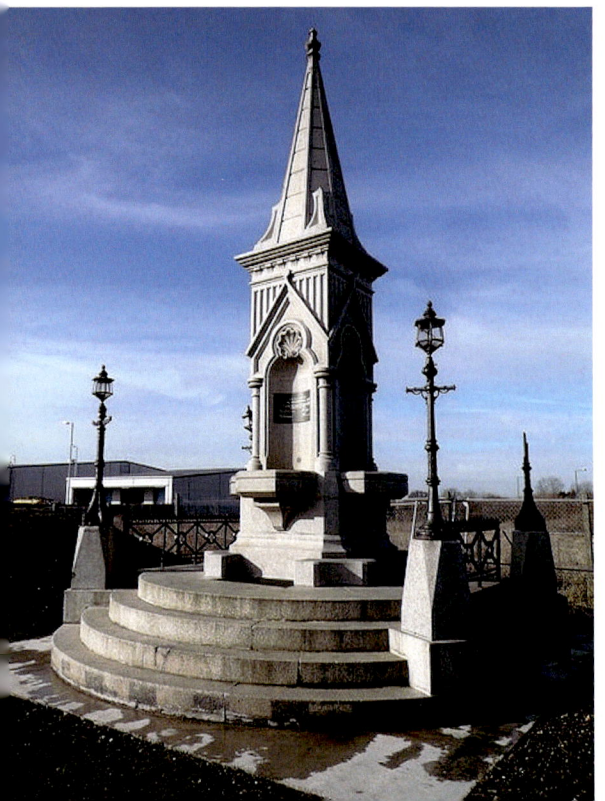

The ornate drinking fountain that once stood by Kew Bridge, now at Western International Market. (J. Taylor under Creative Commons)

G

Gas

One of the first gasworks in the world was established at Brentford, in 1820. It was not pretty. Its high, blank walls stretched along either side of the High Street for a quarter of a mile and the works, in which coal brought up the Thames by barge was burned to create coal gas, covered 8.5 acres.

The journalist and novelist Cecil Roberts described the approach to Brentford in a novel of 1940, *And So to Bath*: 'Let us be truthful, the entrance to Brentford is like the gate to Hell. Already the gasworks and coal yards are there for stoking the punishing fires.'

Gas was first produced here to light the road from Kensington to Hounslow but, in 1926, production was greatly expanded to supply households and public utilities over a wide area, stretching from Hammersmith in the east to Windsor in the west, and from Edgeware to Richmond, north to south.

When the gas industry was nationalised in 1949 the work was run by the North Thames Gas Board, but it became redundant when natural gas replaced that produced from coal in 1963. Brentford's street lamps were fuelled by gas until 1960.

George III

For several years from 1772, George III found Kew a peaceful and restorative place. Here he would retreat, king and queen living rather like country gentry, at the White House in Kew Gardens. Life here offered a tranquil contrast to that led at other, grander palaces.

However, in the winter months of 1788–9, the king's mind became severely unbalanced. He was confined to Kew during attacks, but allowed to live at Windsor Castle once they had passed. He was given a couple of ground-floor rooms at the White House, while his doctors and equerries filled a wing. The rooms above George's apartment were kept empty so that his ravings could not be overheard.

As David Blomfield writes in *Kew Past*: 'King George was at times unable to tell a tree from an ambassador. What made those months even more distressing was that

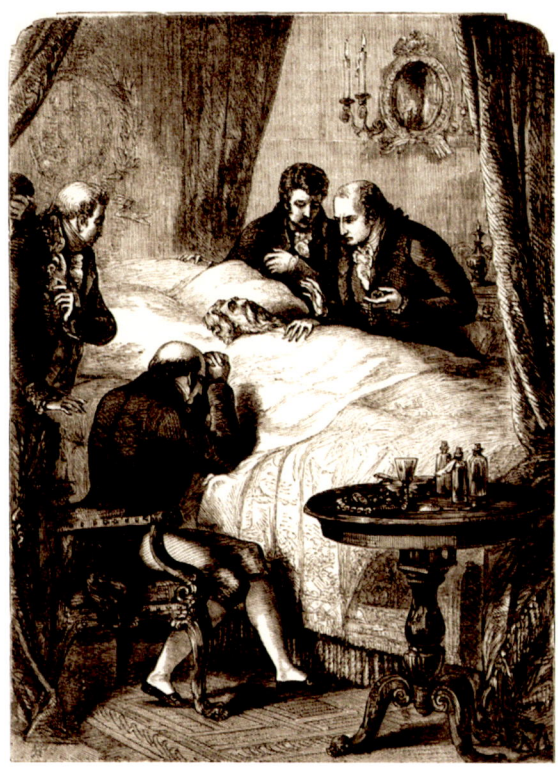

The death of George III.
(John Cassell)

the doctors had no idea of what was wrong, as the king suffered from porphyria, a disease that had not then been recognised.'

Porphyria, in severe cases such as the king's, affects the nervous system and has a range of acute symptoms including anxiety, confusion, hallucinations, and overt psychosis. Blomfield writes:

> In Kew, where he spent most of the nine months of this first attack of the disease, the effect was especially traumatic. The king was known for being a kindly gentleman who would walk out along the towpath, accompanied by just a single equerry, or through the village touching his hat to his subjects, and occasionally subjecting them to embarrassingly detailed enquiries about their circumstances. He was liked – even loved – for his lack of ceremony. Now, however, when he went out for walks he was surrounded by doctors and attendants, and occasionally returned in a straitjacket.

During one of the regular remissions from his illness, George III planned a new residence at Kew. Building began on a Gothic Castellated Palace on the riverside, and the White House was demolished, in 1802. A sundial, placed just west of the present Orangery, marks the spot where it stood. It bears the initials of William III, and was moved here from Kensington Palace by William IV. George's replacement palace was also later demolished.

Great Pagoda, The

The Great Pagoda at Kew Gardens is an elegant folly that also came to serve an unexpected practical purpose. It was created in 1761 by Sir William Chambers as a present for Princess Augusta, the founder of the gardens. The design reflects the burgeoning interest in Chinese art and culture resulting from greatly increased trade between China and Great Britain at the time.

It stands 163 feet tall, and 253 steps lead up through its ten storeys to a viewing gallery. It is decorated with eighty dragons covered in coloured glass and carrying bells in their mouths.

The building was intended to be entirely decorative but, during the Second World War, it was used to test the aerodynamic characteristics of smoke bombs. Holes were cut in the floors so that weapons under development could be dropped down the building.

By the end of the last century the Pagoda was in a dilapidated state. A major restoration project was undertaken in which the dragons, many of them by then missing, were re-carved using one of the surviving originals as a model.

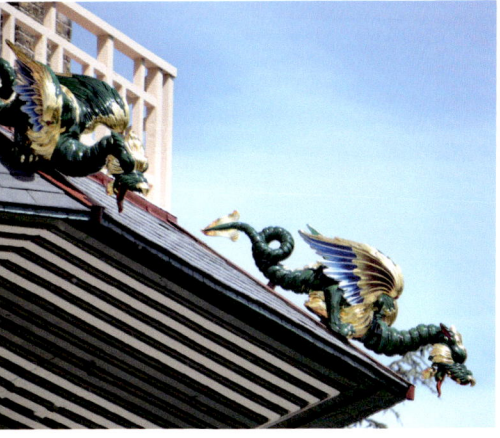

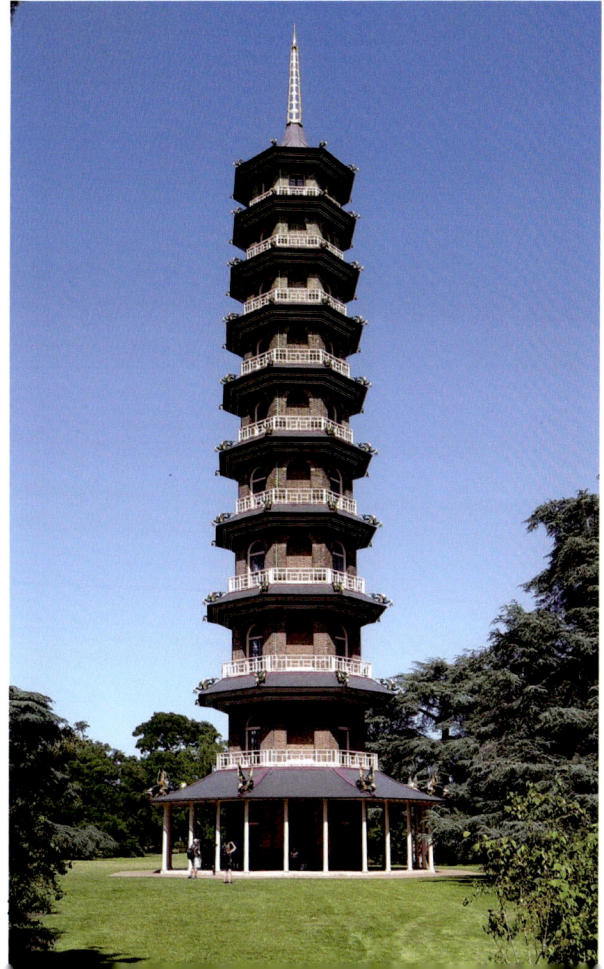

Above and right: The Great Pagoda at Kew Gardens. (Mx Granger and Andy Scott under Creative Commons)

Grey, Lady Jane

England's queen with the shortest reign once lived at Syon House. It was here, in July 1553, on the death of Henry VIII's son, Edward VI, that Lady Jane Grey, the sixteen-year-old grand-daughter of Henry, was offered the crown.

Syon was owned by John Dudley, Duke of Northumberland, and Jane was married to his son, Lord Guildford Dudley. The duke, in his role as Lord Protector, made the offer of the crown, which Jane only accepted with great reluctance.

The more natural heir was Mary Tudor, Henry's daughter, but she was a Catholic and Northumberland judged that she would have little popular support. Jane was taken downriver to London and proclaimed queen. Her reign lasted just nine days before she was displaced by Mary Tudor. She was executed the following year, as was Northumberland.

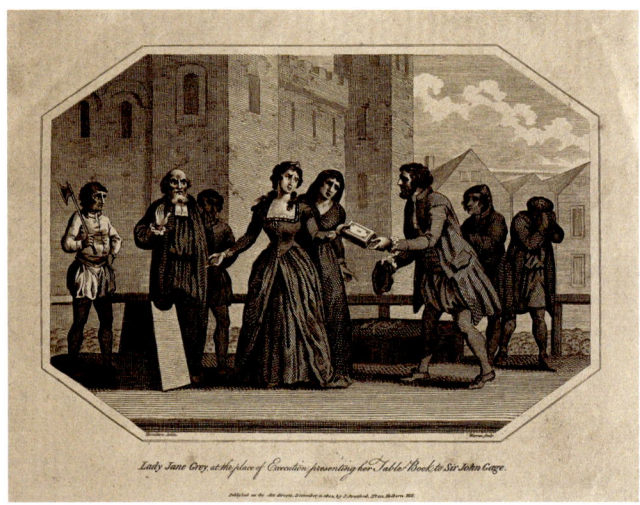

Left and below: Lady Jane Grey, portrayed at her execution, once lived at Syon House. (Wellcome Collection and Maxwell Hamilton under Creative Commons)

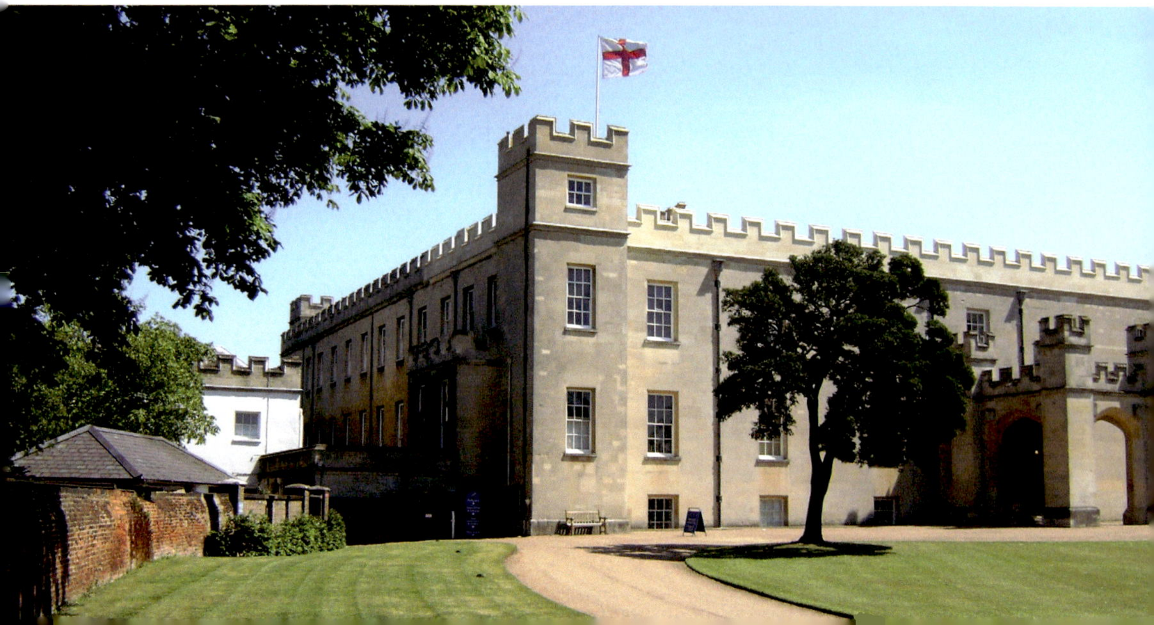

Griffin

The symbol of the griffin has a long association with Brentford. The legend is that Nell Gwyn, mistress of Charles II, lived at Brent House on the corner of Upper Butts and Brent Road. Here she kept a pet griffin, which one day fell into the River Brent and was presumed drowned.

However, the mythical winged creature survived, climbing out of the water at Brentford Eyot. There it remained for many years, griffins being incredibly long-lived. It found a mate, supposedly, when Sir Joseph Banks brought one back from a Pacific island, visited on one of his flora- and fauna-hunting expeditions, and housed it in the Pagoda in Kew Gardens.

This griffin escaped and flew to the eyot, where the pair founded a whole colony of griffins that spread out all over Brentford. There are those that say you can still spot the shy creatures today, if you look hard enough.

The connection with Griffin Park, former home to Brentford Football Club, comes from the fact that the team's home ground from 1903 until 2020, when they moved to the Brentford (now G-Tech) Community Stadium, was built on an orchard owned by Fuller, Smith and Turner. The firm brews its beers at the Griffin Brewery in Chiswick, and its symbol is a griffin.

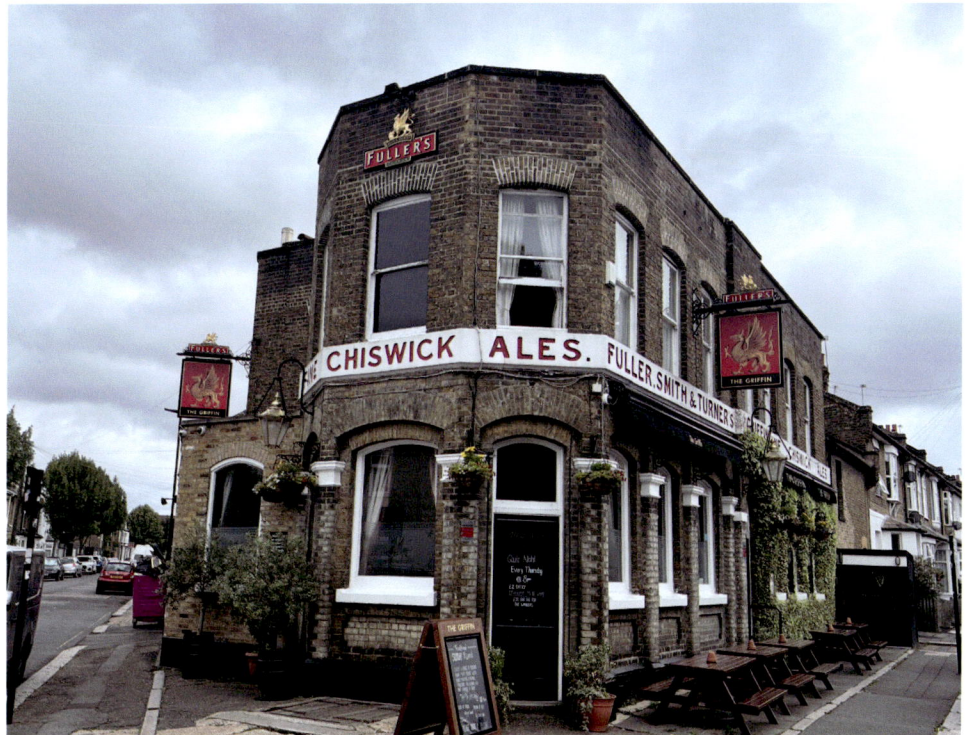

The Griffin pub, once Brentford FC's clubhouse.

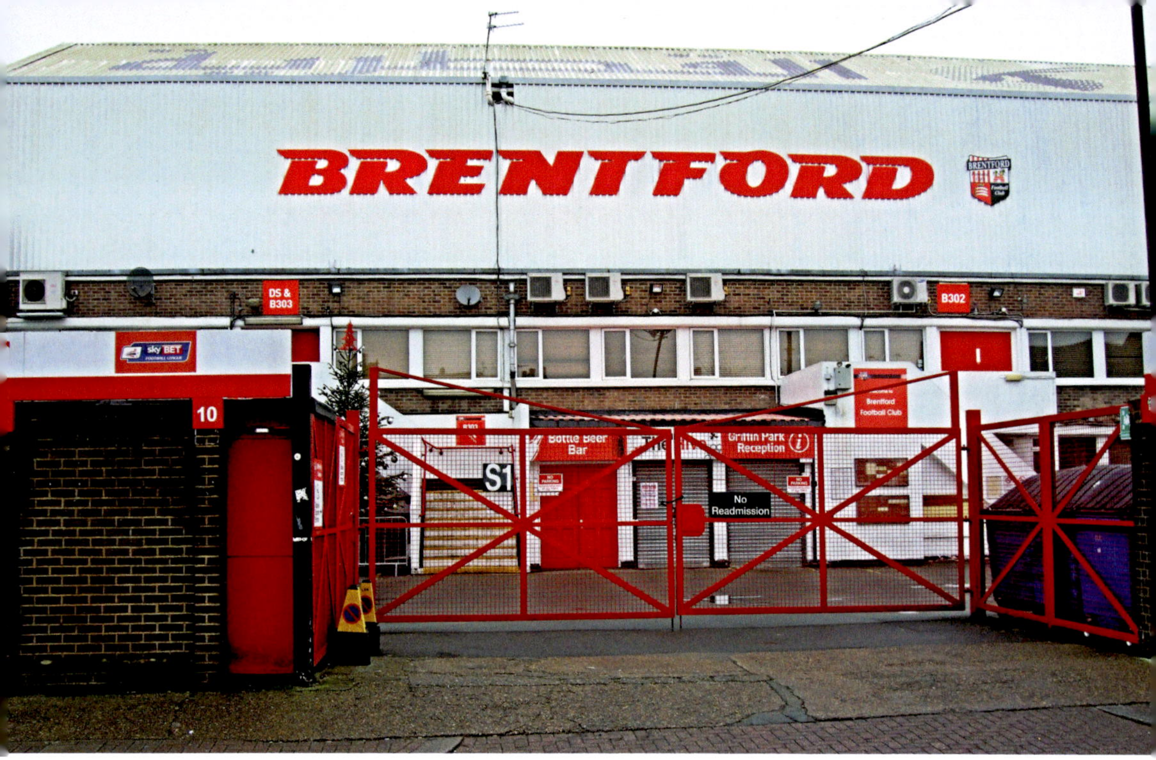

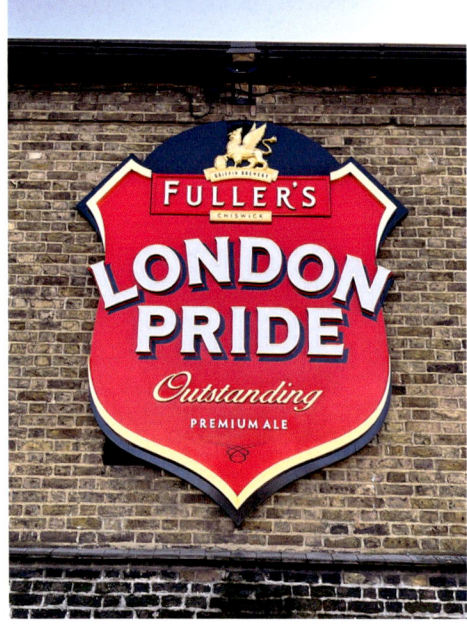

Above: Griffin Park, former home of Brentford FC. (Jim Linwood under Creative Commons)

Left: The Griffin emblem is used on Fuller's beers.

    The griffin is an impressive creature. It has the tail, back legs and torso of a lion, the head and wings of an eagle, and sometimes an eagle's talons on its front feet.
    Another legend associated with Nell Gwyn is that Charles once rode his horse into Brent House and up the stairs, determined to see Nell after a row in which she broke off relations. The house was demolished in 1909.

H

HMS *Bounty*

In 1788, two Kew gardeners sailed on HMS *Bounty* to Tahiti and collected over 1,000 breadfruit trees. When the ship sailed on the crew, led by Fletcher Christian, mutinied.

One of them was David Nelson, a gardener and botanist who had previously sailed on James Cook's unsuccessful four-year voyage to discover the Northwest Passage and hence sail from the Atlantic to the Pacific Ocean along Canada's arctic coast.

On the *Bounty*, Nelson was responsible for 1,015 breadfruit trees which had been placed in pots and were intended for transfer to the West Indies where commercial crops of this fruit, a staple in tropical regions, would be grown.

When the crew of the *Bounty* mutinied, Nelson remained loyal to Captain Bligh and was one of nineteen men set adrift in a small boat, which undertook a remarkable 3,800-mile voyage to the Indonesian island of Timor. He survived the epic journey but, sadly, died of a fever a few days after reaching land in 1789. Bligh later named Mount Nelson, in Tasmania, Australia, in the botanist's honour.

Hooker, Sir William

William Hooker became the first full-time director of Kew Gardens in 1841, when it was decided it would prosper by being taken out of royal hands, placed under state ownership and run as a botanic garden.

It was a post he had long coveted. Hooker (1785–1865) had extensive experience in both academic and practical botany. He had published an account of an expedition to Iceland in 1809, and later became Regius Professor of Botany at Glasgow University, where he established the Royal Botanic Institution of Glasgow and laid out and developed the city's botanic gardens.

When he got the job at Kew he wrote: 'I feel as if I were to begin life over again,' and quickly set about expanding the gardens from the modest 11 acres it had covered for most of its first eighty years. In a few years the gardens grew to cover 300 acres.

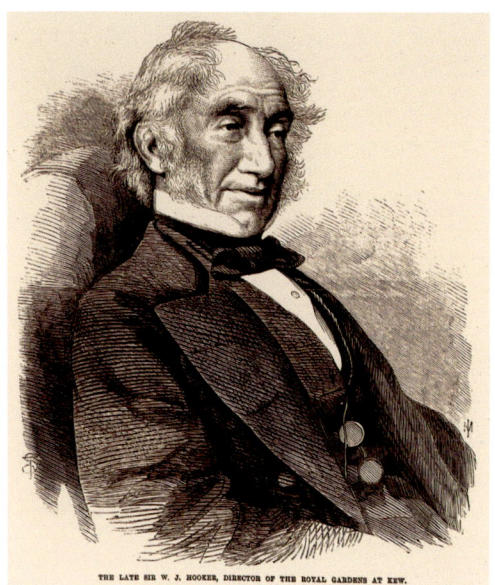 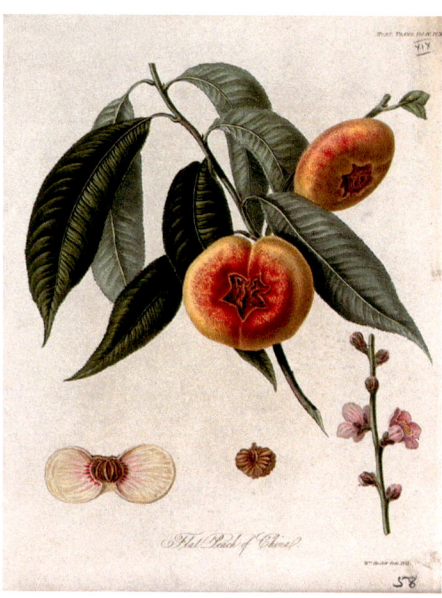

Above left and above right: Sir William Hooker, and one of his etchings of a specimen. (Wellcome Collection)

An arboretum was created and the Palm House, built in 1843. The layout of the gardens was transformed, with new vistas offering views of the Pagoda and across the Thames to Syon House, and the Broad Walk leading to Kew Palace (originally known as the Dutch House) laid out. For the first time, the public were able to freely explore the grounds, which were open daily, and Hooker often wandered among the visitors – who included Queen Victoria and Prince Albert – answering questions and offering his expertise.

Scientific work also expanded rapidly, as did Kew's collections of plants and seeds. Sir William developed good relations with other botanic gardens, generously sharing cuttings and seeds, and receiving many donations in return. He established a museum of economic botany, which explores the relationship between plants and people.

Hooker made his home at West Hall, in West Hall Road, Kew, where his collection of plants and books filled thirteen rooms. The house survives, Kew's only remaining seventeenth-century buildings apart from Kew Palace.

Thanks to Sir William, the Royal Botanic Gardens at Kew became the centre of a worldwide network of botanic expertise, exploration, discovery and scholarship.

When Sir William Hooker died, he was buried in St Anne's Church on Kew Green, and his son Joseph succeeded him as director.

I

Impressionism

A number of artists have spent time in Kew, including the father of Impressionism, Camille Pissarro (1830–1903). He came to lodge at a house on Kew Green in 1892, towards the end of his life, and painted a number of local scenes, including Kew Green and Kew Gardens.

However, it was not the scenery that was his prime reason for being here. As David Blomfield writes in *Kew Past*:

> He had come to Kew to sort out a domestic difficulty. His son Lucien was living in England [in Chiswick] and had fallen in love with a Jewess, whose parents were set against the match. After long discussions with Camille they reluctantly allowed the wedding to go ahead.

Industry

Some of the finest industrial buildings in the country once lined Brentford's Golden Mile, a stretch of the new Great West Road, opened by George V in 1925 and designed to remove traffic from jammed-up Brentford High Street.

The Golden Mile ran from the Chiswick roundabout to the junction with Syon Lane, at what became known as Gillette Corner, where the razor blade company built an imposing factory with a 150-foot clock tower. This stretch of road is actually 2 miles long.

Major companies flocked to build prestigious new headquarters and factories in the then hugely fashionable art deco style. They included the Firestone tyre company; Smith's Crisps; Beecham pharmaceuticals; Currys; Coty perfumes; MacLeans toothpaste; Jantzen swimwear; Trico-Folberth windscreen wipers; the Pyrene Fire Extinguisher company; and the Sperry Gyroscope Company, which made ship guidance systems.

There were several car firms, including Alvis and the American marques Lincoln and Packard, and a showroom for Henly's, selling Jaguars and Studebakers.

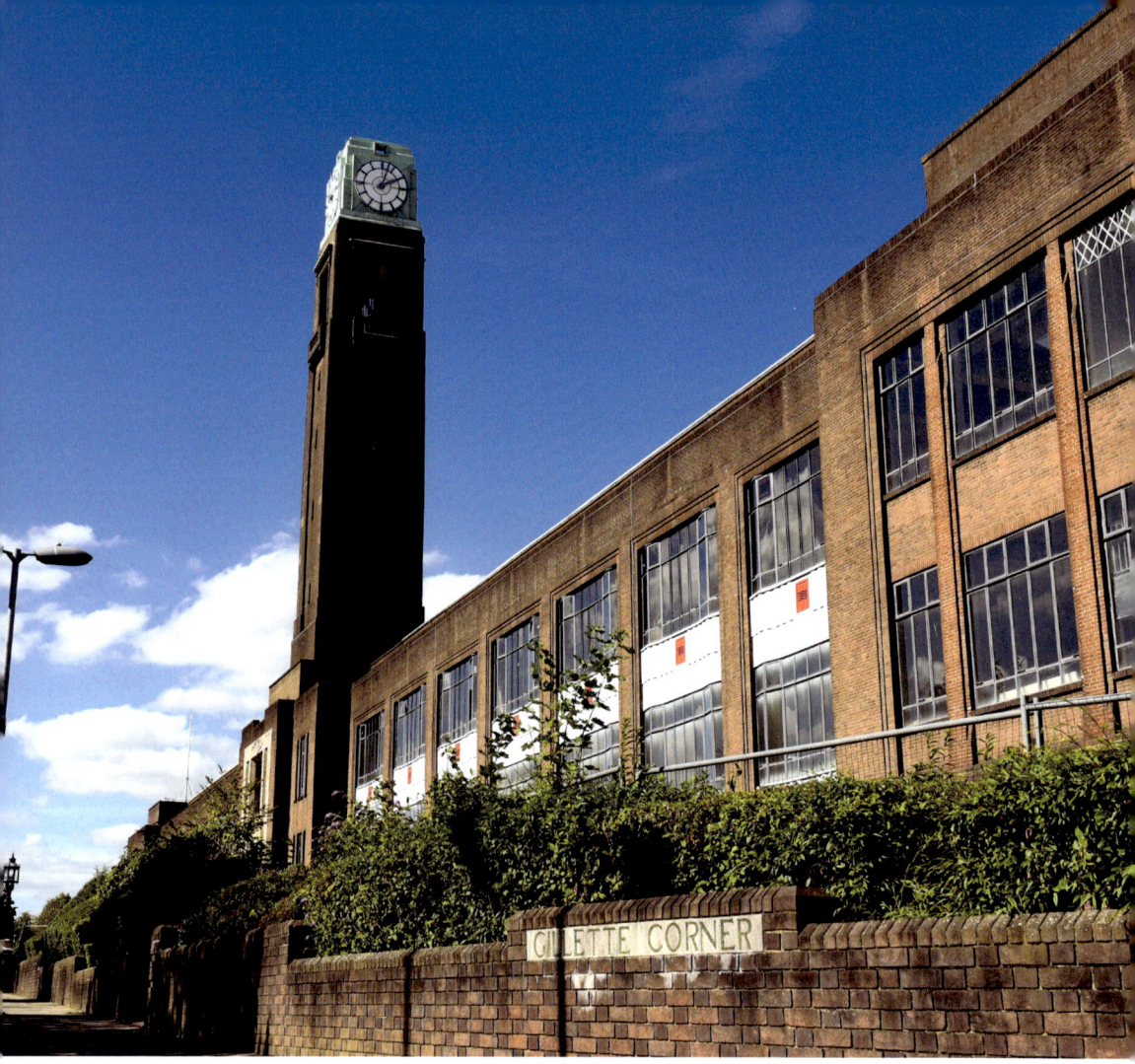

Above and opposite: Three survivors on Brentford's Golden Mile: former homes to Gillette, Coty and Currys. (StewartK, West London Dweller and Kt0288 under Creative Commons)

To the writer J. B. Priestley it 'looked very odd. Being new it did not look English. We might suddenly have rolled into California.'

From the 1960s the architectural coherence of the Golden Mile began to crumble as such firms moved away, their premises were demolished and new buildings in a wide range of styles replaced them.

Today, only a handful of original art deco factories survive: those created for Coty, at No. 941, now offices; Currys, at No. 991, now occupied by advertising company JC Decaux; Simmonds Aerocessories, later occupied by the BOAC airline and Beecham, now redeveloped as apartments and topped with the name of the builder, Barratt; and Gillette, currently unoccupied.

Each Christmas, up until the 1990s, the firms made great efforts to decorate their premises with lights and trees, making Brentford's Golden Mile something of a tourist attraction.

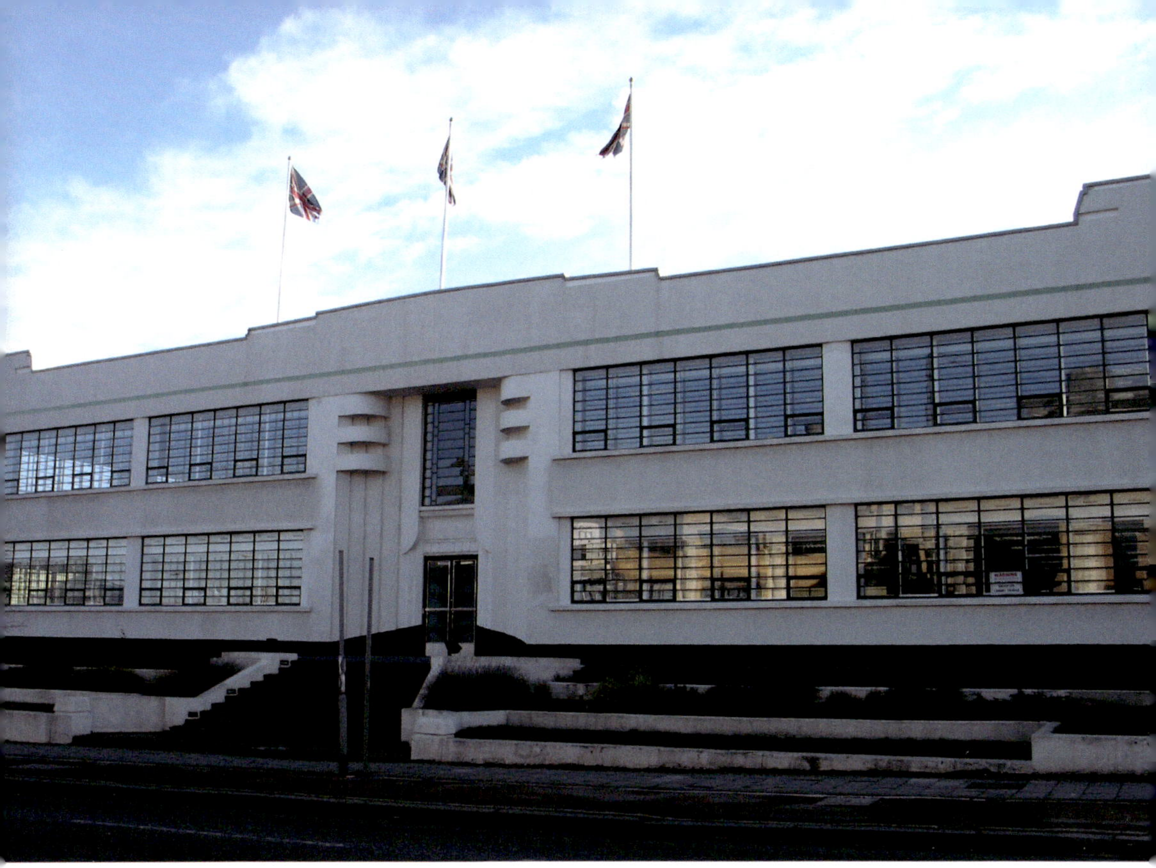

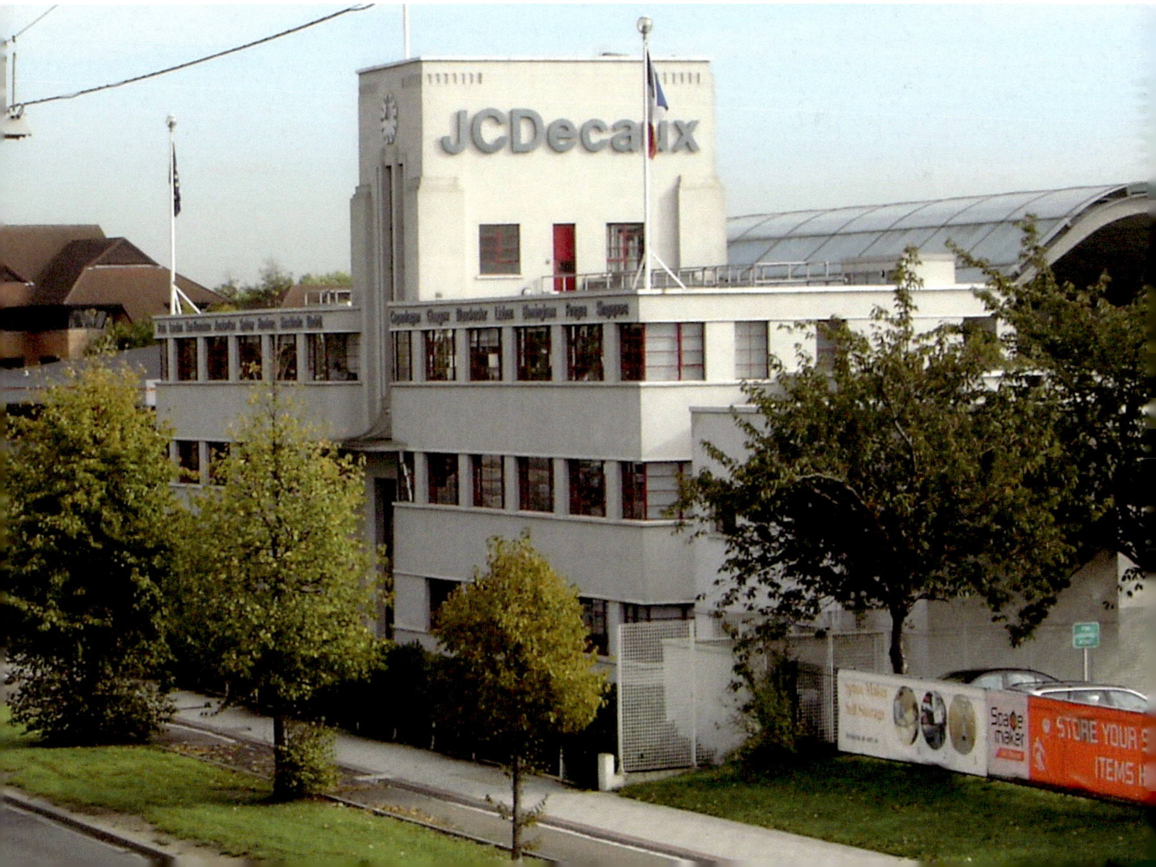

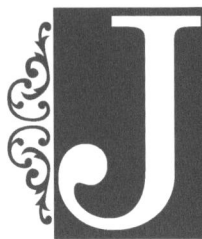

Jam

Today, Brentford is probably most famous for its Premiership football team. A hundred and fifty years ago, the town was famous for jam.

Thomas Beach's jams achieved world renown. In 1867, he took a lease on 26 acres of orchards stretching along either side of the Ealing Road. Forty employees boiled up pears, plums, blackcurrants, strawberries and other fruits in a factory between Walnut Tree Road and Cressage Road. Any fruits too damaged for jam were turned into wine.

It had taken Thomas Beach many years to reach this level of success. Janet McNamara writes, in *Beach's of Brentford: The World Famous Jam*:

> In 1851 a young man called Thomas William Beach won prizes for his British Queen Strawberries at Covent Garden, from Chiswick Horticultural Society and at the Great Exhibition in Hyde Park. Some of his fruits weighed in at 4oz each.

Strawberries were Beach's particular passion, and he named his home, which stood on the corner of his factory site, Strawberry Villa. The house was decorated with carvings of strawberry fruit and leaves.

By the 1880s Beach had gained a national reputation, and by 1901 T. W. Beach and company's jams had won seventeen medals for excellence. Captain Scott took Beach's jam on his ill-fated expedition to the South Pole.

Thomas Beach was a benevolent employer, who provided a theatre for his staff. Janet McNamara writes:

> The theatre was a philanthropic gesture on the part of Mr Beach designed to keep his workforce out of the many public houses in the area. Admission was one old penny or two empty jam jars, obviously an early form of recycling. In later years he supplied soup and bread to needy people of the town during bad winters.

As demand spiralled, Beach's found they needed far more fruit than could be grown in Brentford. Extra was supplied by family members from a string of orchards across west London, and on 500 acres on Lord Sudeley's estate at Sudeley Castle near Cheltenham. Additional factories were established at Evesham and Pershore.

The spread of housing across Brentford meant expansion – and fruit growing – were increasingly difficult here and so, in 1929, the firm moved to larger premises in Hanworth. In 1941 Beach's was taken over by the Unilever conglomerate.

Jewish Settlement

There is a story, disputed by many, believed by some, that in the early eighteenth century a group of jews offered to buy the entire town of Brentford, with the aim of creating a ghetto.

The offer is said to have been made to Lord Godolphin, Lord Treasurer of England under William III and Queen Anne. Jews were expelled from England in 1290 and only allowed to return by Cromwell in 1656. They were, however, viewed with suspicion by some, and envy for their ability to prosper.

Below and overleaf: Gunnersbury House and Park, home of Lionel Rothschild, the first Jewish member of parliament.

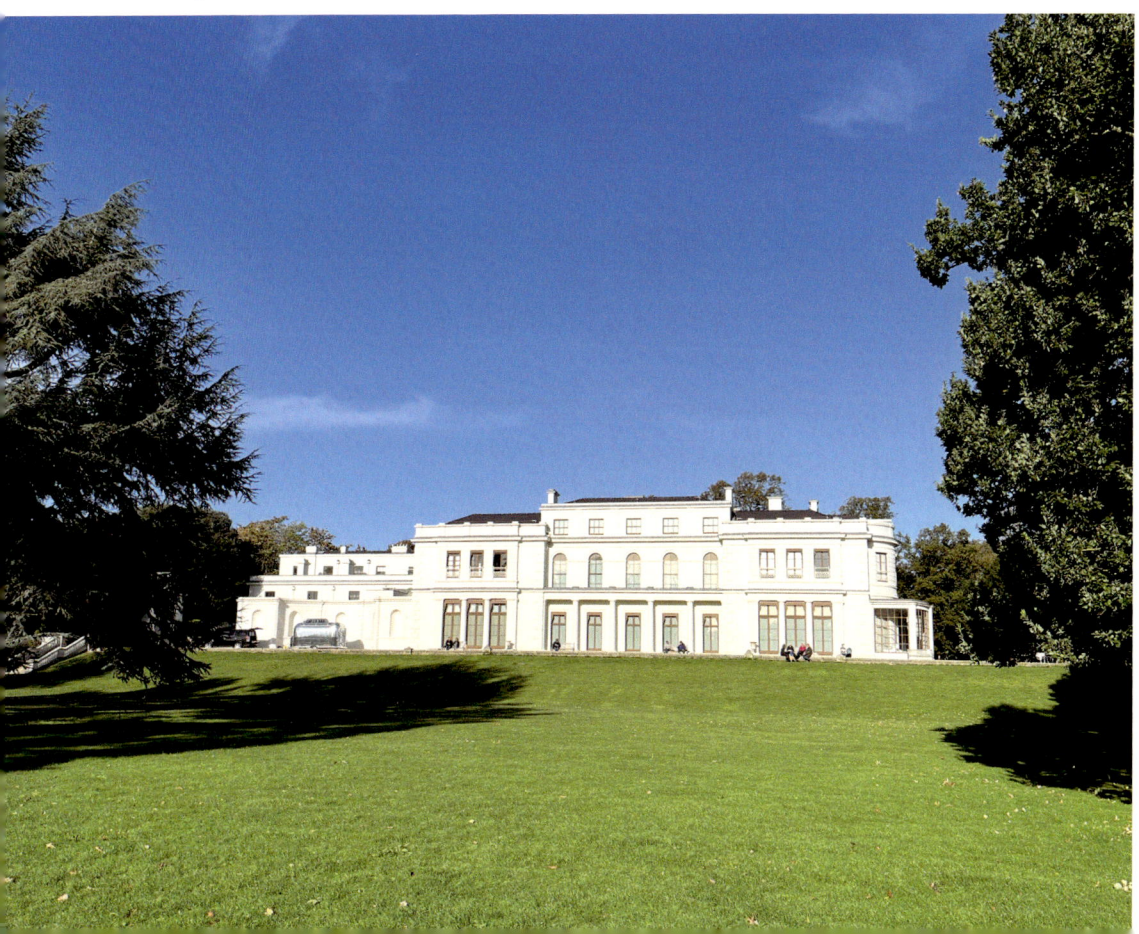

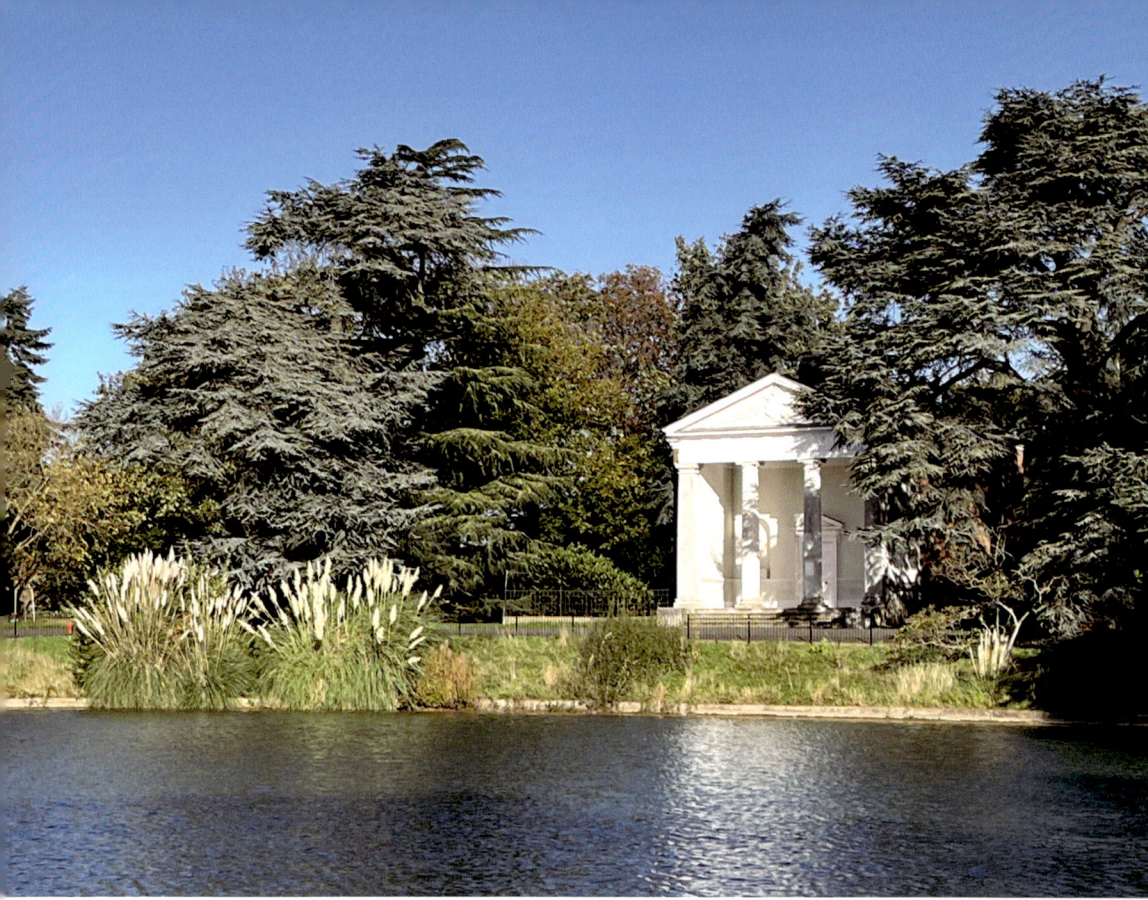

The story may originate in fear of these very able immigrants, and there were similar false stories about their ambitions, such as a supposed offer to buy St Paul's Cathedral for £1 million and convert it into a synagogue. Gillian Clegg writes, in *Brentford Past*:

> There are those, however, who think the plan to turn Brentford into a super ghetto could be genuine. They point to the fact that many Jewish people settled in west London at the beginning of the eighteenth century, notably Moses Hart who lived in Gordon House, Isleworth between 1718 and 1756. Hart was immensely wealthy and built a new synagogue in the City of London.

Certainly, Brentford became home to one of the most eminent Jewish families, the Rothschilds, of Gunnersbury House. Lionel Rothschild became the first Jewish member of parliament, representing the City of London, in 1847.

K

Kangaroos

Exotic animals including the first kangaroos to arrive in Britain were once kept in a menagerie in the gardens at Kew. The animals were kept in a paddock alongside Queen Charlotte's Cottage, established in 1792.

There were also buffaloes and quagga (a now extinct sub-species of zebra), black swans and colourful Tartarian pheasants. The cottage, hidden away in 300-year-old bluebell woods, may have begun life as a home for the keeper of the menagerie, and was later expanded and given to Queen Charlotte as a wedding gift on her marriage to George III, in 1761. She enjoyed afternoon tea and picnics here. The cottage was given to the public by Queen Victoria in 1898.

Kew

There are a couple of possible origins of the name Kew. One theory is that it is probably derived from the Saxon 'key-hough', which means the wood or 'hough' by the quay. Another theory is that Kew's original name was Cayho or Cyho, deriving from the Old French *kai* meaning the 'cay' or quay, and the old English 'hoh' or 'ho', a spur of

All four seasons in one at Kew. From left: spring, summer, autumn and winter. (James Morley under Creative Commons)

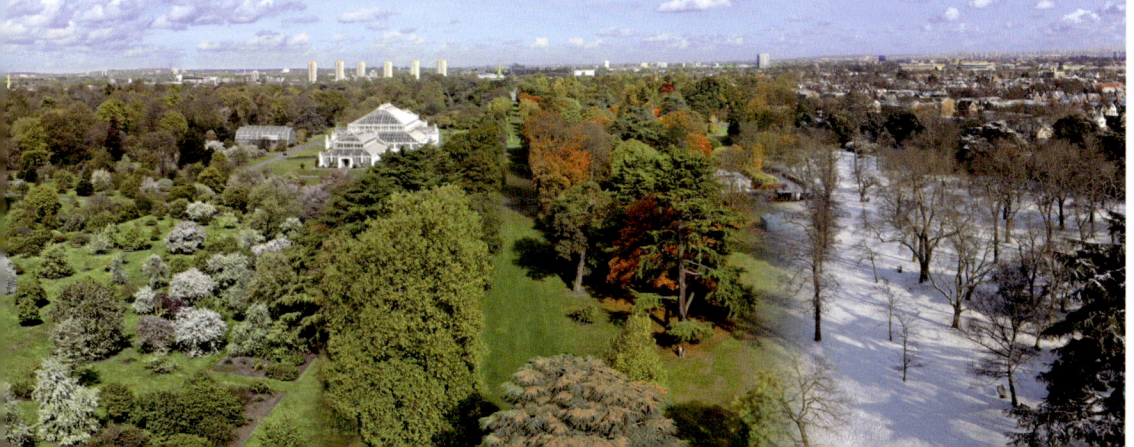

land, the spur in this case being formed by a bend in the Thames. There were in fact over twenty variants on the name until Kew came into general use in the seventeenth century.

That spur of land is today a broad peninsula defined by the river: the Thames running north, then arcing west and finally south around Kew.

Kew Bridge

Before the eighteenth century there were no bridges over the Thames between London Bridge and Kingston Bridge. Then six additional, intervening bridges were built. The third of those was at Kew.

This first Kew Bridge was wooden and built by Robert Tunstall, a Brentford businessman. When it opened in 1759 it was the sole bridge across the Thames on the stretch from Fulham to Kingston, and such a novelty that 3,000 people crossed on its opening day. Tolls were 1s 6d (7.5p) for a coach and horses, a halfpenny for pedestrians.

In 1774, the bridge came to grief when a boat collided with it, causing substantial damage, and it was closed for two years. Robert Tunstall's son (also Robert) then replaced it with a stone bridge.

By the end of the nineteenth century the bridge could not cope with the volume of traffic using it, and it was replaced with the present bridge, designed by Sir John Wolfe Barry, who was also responsible for the far showier Tower Bridge, in 1903.

Kew Bridge. (ZeevoX under Creative Commons)

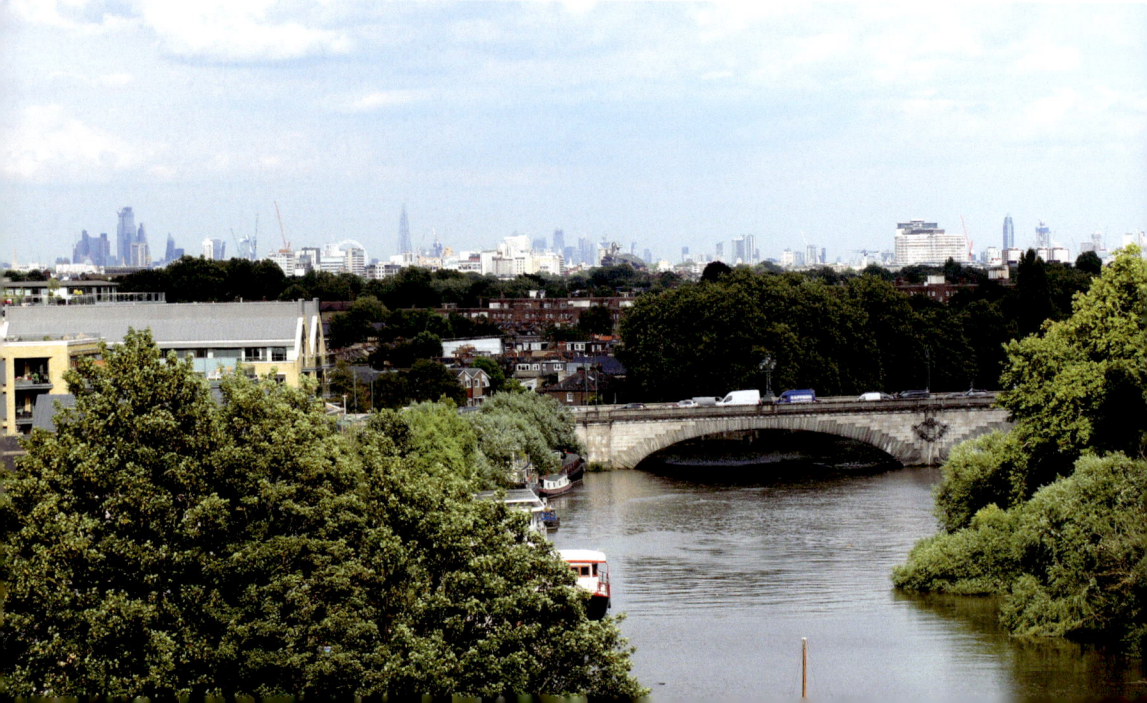

Kew's First Gardeners

William Turner (1509–68), a doctor and clergyman with a deep interest in botany, became the first person to garden seriously at Kew.

Turner was employed by the Duke of Somerset, who lived at Syon House, as his chaplain and personal physician, but became hugely frustrated that all his time was taken up with medicine rather than botany. He had a house in Kew where he cultivated a large garden but wrote that, in three and a half years, he had just three weeks to, as he put it, 'bestowe upon ye seekyng of herbes, and markyng in what places they grow'.

In 1551 Turner published the first part of his *A New Herball, wherin are conteyned the names of herbes*, in which it is clear that he grew many plants in his garden, the location of which is sadly unknown. It is highly appropriate that the man who became known as the Father of Botany should have done much of his research in Kew, the home of botanic study and exploration.

This and two subsequent volumes, published in 1562 and 1568, gave the first comprehensive, accessible survey of English plants, illustrated with woodcuts that made them easily recognisable. It also itemised their 'uses and vertues'. For the first time, thanks to Turner, the ordinary person had access to a comprehensive guide to natural medicines and remedies, written in English. In his preface he says that there were those who believed such information should be kept the closely guarded secrets of the medical profession.

The first royal gardener at Kew was Prince Frederick (1707–51), eldest son of George II and father of George III. His untimely death at the age of forty-four prevented him acceding to the throne. Instead, Kew Gardens is his lasting legacy. As David Blomfield writes in *Kew Past*, 'Without his enthusiasm the garden would never have taken the course it did.'

His particular interest was in exotic plants rather than elaborate landscapes and, together with his wife, Augusta, and John Stuart, Earl of Bute, he laid out the plans for a major botanic garden. His interest in the gardens may have killed him. His doctor put the cause of his death down to catching a fatal cold while standing in the rain watching trees being planted.

Kew Green

The 33-acre triangle of Kew Green provides a welcome green lung for travellers grinding north or south through Brentford and Kew.

Despite the South Circular Road slicing through it, there is still something of the atmosphere of a village green about the place, with its cricket pitch, pond, St Anne's Church and a number of pubs and restaurants facing onto it. Cricket has been played here since the 1730s, and it is still home to the local Kew Cricket Club. A horticultural show, held each August, enhances the village-green atmosphere.

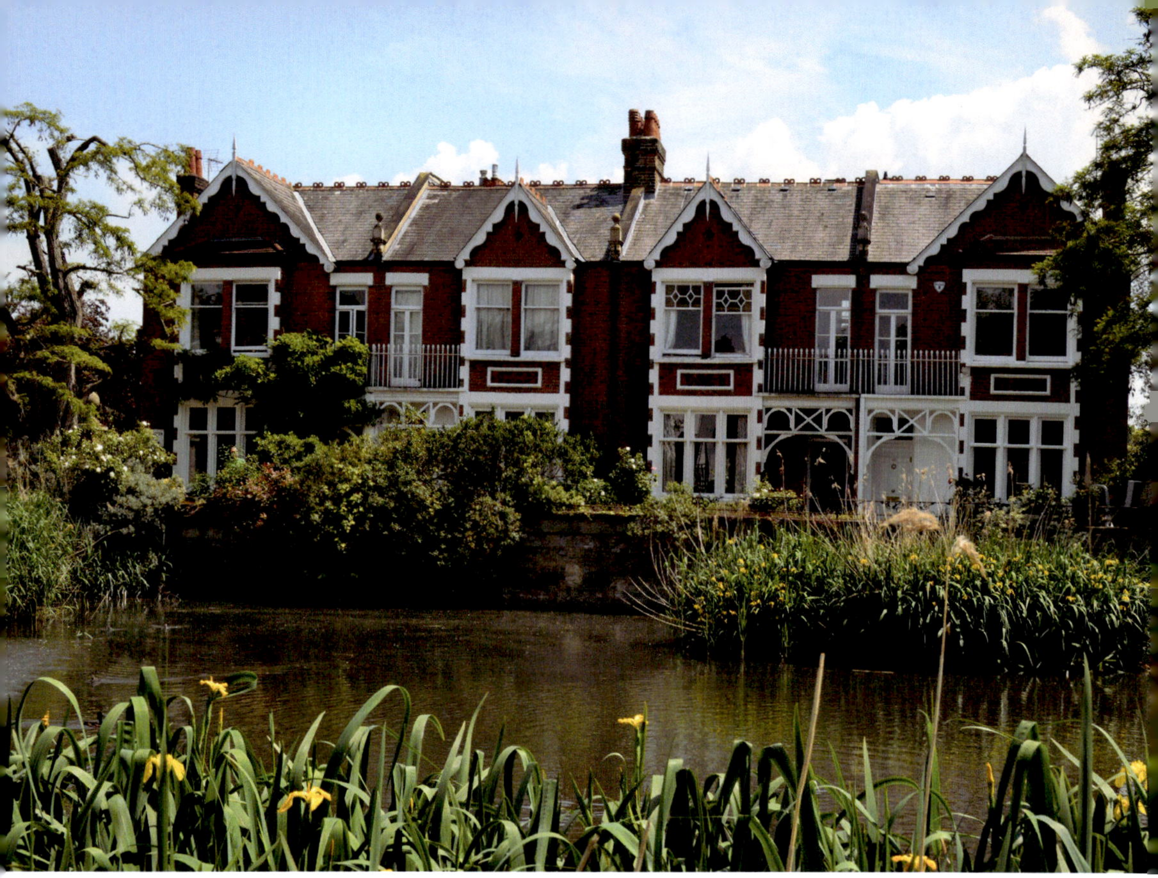

Above and below: Kew Green: the pond, and The Greyhound pub. (Andy Scott under Creative Commons)

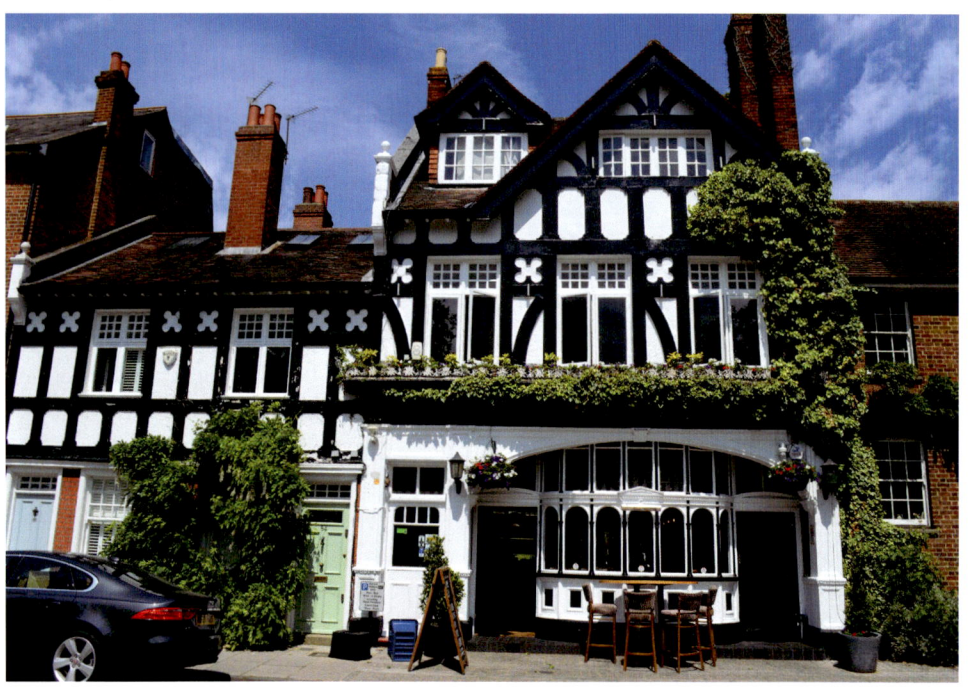

Kew Pond, once appreciated by thirsty horses hauling loads across the green, may have originally been a natural pond fed from a creek leading to the Thames. During high spring tides, sluice gates are opened to allow water from the river to flow into the pond via an underground pipe. The pond now has a concrete base, but is maintained by volunteers who have planted up the island and banks, creating a haven for water birds.

The green has had royal residents. George III bought Cambridge Cottage, tucked in a corner close to Kew Gardens, as a home for two of his sons and, in 1838, his seventh son, the Duke of Cambridge (1774–1850), extended the house. The Duchess of Cambridge (1797–1889) also lived here, leaving the house to her son, Prince George, Duke of Cambridge (1819–1904) on her death. When George died, in 1904, it passed to Kew Gardens, and can now be hired for corporate and other events.

David Blomfield, in *Kew Past*, notes that in the 1770s–80s the green was a mecca for musicians. He writes:

> George III loved organ music … and the rest of the royal family also played instruments. The royal concert master had a distinguished pedigree of his own. He was Johann Christian Bach, the youngest son of Johann Sebastian Bach, and with other court musicians would practice in houses around Kew Green.

A number of artists have lived on the green, most distinguished among them being one of our finest portrait and landscape painters, Thomas Gainsborough (1727–88). He was a favourite of George III and his sons and regularly visited them at Kew, staying with his friend, Joshua Kirby, drawing master to the royal family. After Kirby's death he continued to visit, renting No. 25 Kew Green. Gainsborough chose to be buried at St Anne's Church, just across the green from this house, alongside his friend.

Not all Kew Green inhabitants were among the great and the good. One was a robber and house-breaker called Mr Fame, who was often placed in the village stocks that stood alongside St Anne's. When he wasn't in them he liked to sit alongside them, drinking beer with his friends. Yet, wrote the local diarist Mrs Papendiek, 'we all spoke with him as a friend'. Perhaps he was, because, as she relates, he did not seem to target Kew residents and said: 'If I can take my beer on the green, and sit with my neighbours, I shall take care that no harm happen here.'

Kew Green is owned by the Crown Estate and leased to Richmond upon Thames borough council, which maintains it.

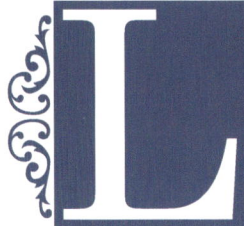

Lucozade Sign

One landmark now sadly missing from alongside the A4 and M4 elevated section is the Lucozade sign. For fifty years, from 1954 to 2004, this neon advertising hording featured, below the word Lucozade, a bottle which poured yellow bubbles of the glucose drink into a glass. A slogan lit up: 'Aids recovery'. This was changed to 'Replaces lost energy' in the 1980s.

Passing it told Brentfordians travelling in from the west that they were home.

The drink, largely carbonated water and glucose syrup, was invented in 1927 by a Newcastle pharmacist, William Walker Hunter, who ran a company called W. Owen & Son. He marketed it as Glucozade. In 1938 the brand was bought by Beecham, the pharmaceuticals company with headquarters on the Great West Road in Brentford, and rechristened Lucozade.

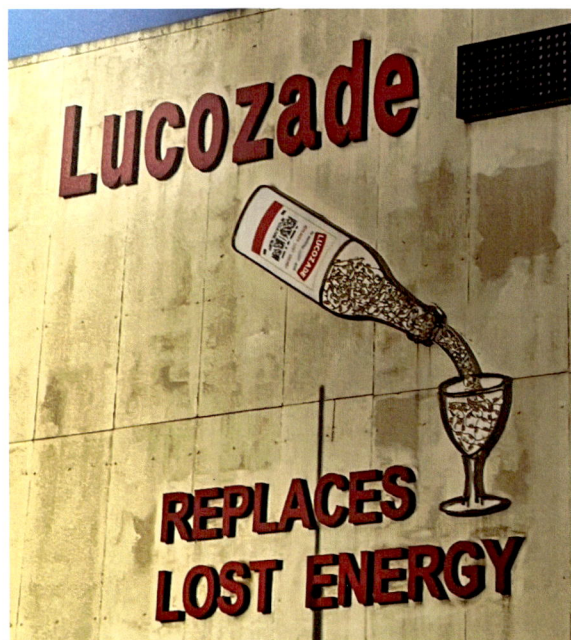

Left and opposite: The Lucozade sign is now gone, but part of it survives in Gunnersbury Park Museum. (Gunnersbury Park Museum)

L

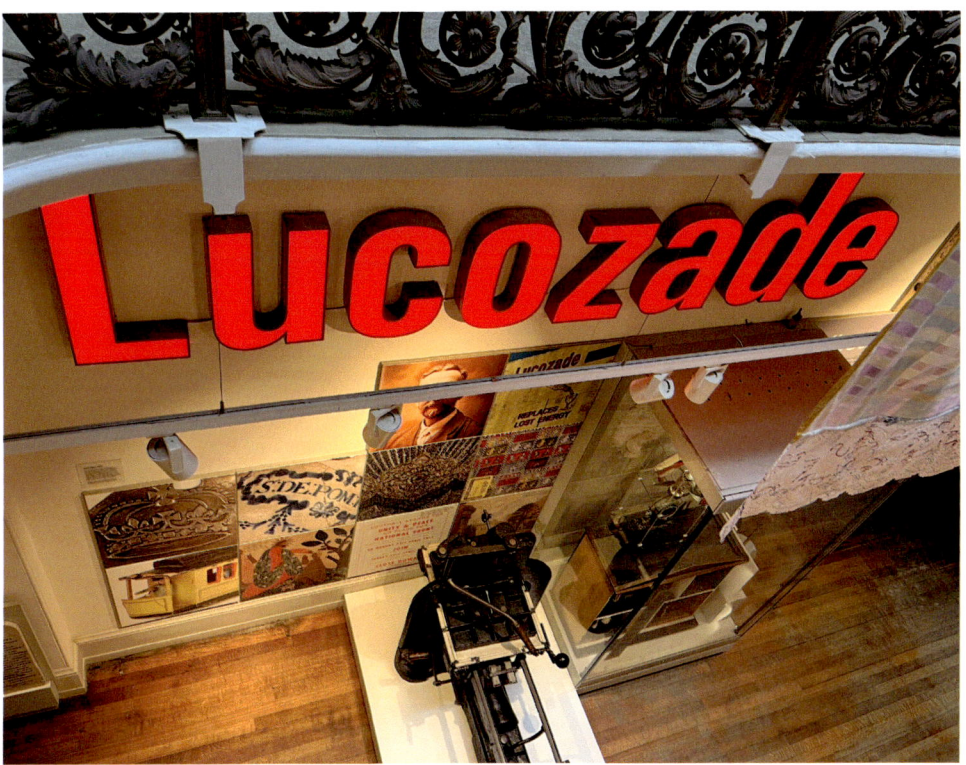

In 2004 the building to which the sign was attached, known as the Beecham Annex, was demolished. In 2010 a digital replica was created and placed on the side of York Parade, 200 yards from the original location. That was replaced in 2015 by a conventional advertising hoarding. Part of the original sign is now in Gunnersbury Park Museum.

Beecham originally marketed the drink as a fortifier for the sick, the clear glass bottle wrapped in yellow cellophane. It was rebranded as a pick-me-up in 1978 and as a sports drink in a plastic bottle in 1983.

Six years later, Beecham merged with a rival to become SmithKline Beecham and, in 2000, with another to become GlaxoSmithKline (GSK). The former Beecham headquarters building (since 1955) was sold for residential development and an imposing new black-glass global headquarters built just to the west.

The Lucozade brand, together with another Beecham stalwart, Ribena, was sold to the Japanese firm Suntory in 2013.

There were many protests at the loss of the original sign. The actress Jennifer Saunders tweeted her disapproval, writing: 'Drove in to London tonight. Lucozade replacement is generic hidiousity.' Kirstie Allsopp tweeted: 'What is this madness?!!! Elevated section of the M4 is a huge part of my heritage.'

Even the digital replacement had its fans, and a petition was raised calling for its reinstatement. In 2024 the Brentford connection was severed, and staff moved to a new headquarters in central London.

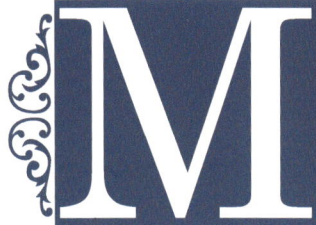

Magistrates' Court, Brentford

The imposing building on Market Square in Brentford was intended to be a town hall. What now houses a restaurant, with apartments above, was built in 1850 as a speculative development by the Brentford Town Hall and Market House Company.

In fact, Brentford decided it didn't want to use it as a town hall and, in 1852, it was leased as a county and magistrates' court. It also housed a library, and a public meeting room. Election results were announced from the balcony above the main entrance.

Before this, courts met in the previous building to occupy this site, the Market House, as did the Local Board, whose twelve members were responsible for health and environmental matters.

Markets were held here for at least 300 years and, by some accounts, from 1306.

Brentford's former magistrates' court.

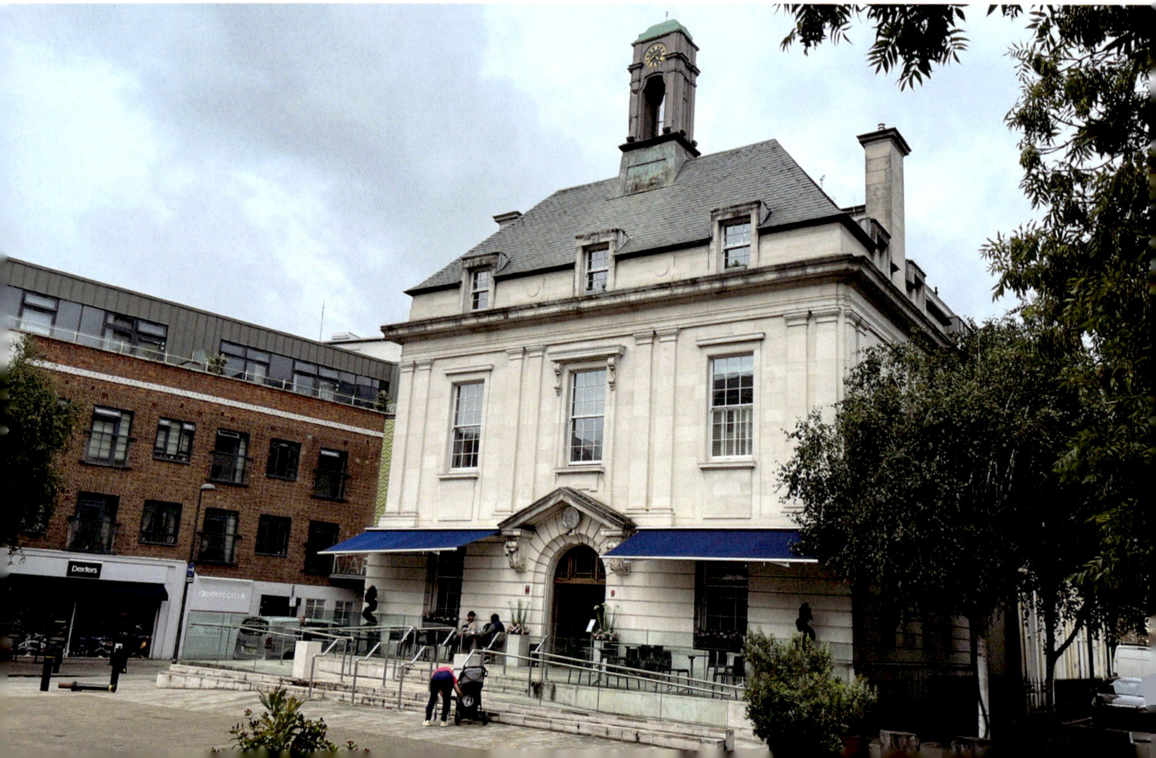

In 1891 the Middlesex County Council bought it to use solely as a court house. The handsome stone frontage was added in 1929, at which time the clock, which had been made by Jullion of Brentford in the eighteenth century and was originally on the old Market House, was moved to the front of the building.

The magistrates' court continued in the Market Place building until 2012, when Ealing Magistrates' Court took over cases from the area, and the building was sold. Markets are once again held on the area in front of the building.

Maids of Honour

Maids of Honour is the name of a Kew cafe and a pastry. Maids of Honour tarts have a puff pastry shell filled with sweetened cheese curds, and are said to have been a favourite of Henry VIII. They are served at the Original Maids of Honour restaurant on Kew Road.

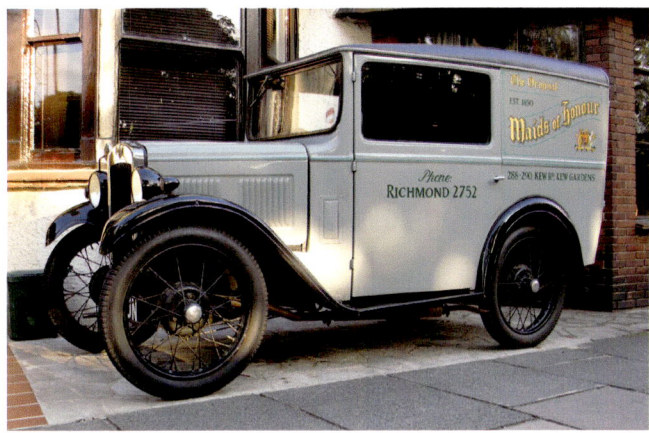

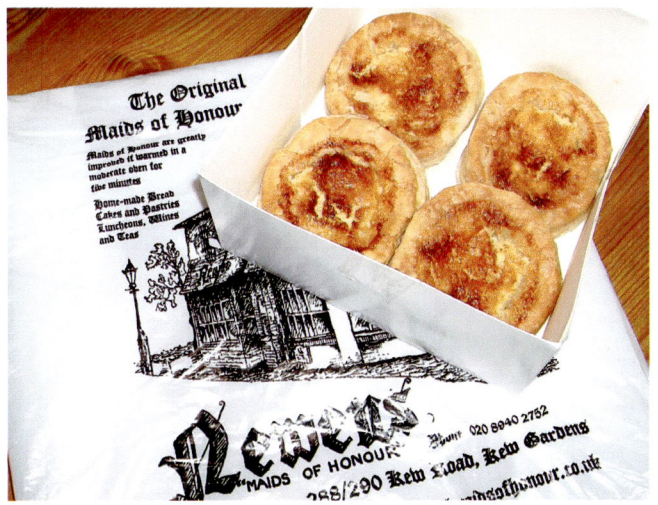

A vintage delivery van at The Maids of Honour cafe, and the pastry after which it is named. (Stefan Czapski and Amanda Slater under Creative Commons)

They were first on sale in the early eighteenth century, at a bakery in Richmond. Robert Newens, an apprentice at the shop, moved a couple of times, taking the recipe with him. Then, 1887, his son Alfred opened the premises on Kew Road from which the tarts have been sold to this day

Maids of Honour was also the name given to the ladies in waiting of Queen Caroline, wife of George II. These ladies were housed in a terrace of four houses, Maids of Honour Row, overlooking Richmond Green.

Martyrs

Six Protestant martyrs were burned at the stake in The Butts in 1558, at a time when England had reverted to Catholicism during the five-year reign of Queen Mary. Under her successor, Elizabeth I, it was Catholics who were martyred for their faith.

The six Brentford martyrs – Robert Milles, Stephen Cotton, Robert Dynes, Stephen Wight, John Slade and William Pikes – were arrested in a raid on a Protestant gathering in north London and imprisoned at the Bishop of London's palace in Fulham. They were later taken at night to Brentford, and then to their death at The Butts.

Following the 1605 Gunpowder Plot, by Catholics including Guy Fawkes, to blow up the Houses of Parliament, bonfires were lit annually in Brentford's streets to mark the anniversary of the foiling of the attempt. From 1748, these were confined solely to The Butts.

Merlin's Cave

When George, Prince of Wales and future George II, bought Richmond Lodge in what is now known as Old Deer Park in 1718, his wife Caroline set about landscaping the grounds. She had William Kent design elaborate follies including Merlin's Cave to add interest to it.

Rather than being designed to look like a cave, this was a large three-roomed cottage with conical, thatched roofs. The two side rooms were fitted with rustic bookcases, the shelves lined with vellum-bound books. The central room featured six life-size waxworks of legendary characters, including Merlin and an assistant, presented at a desk spread with books on magic. It is unclear who the others were meant to represent, though it would make sense if they were also drawn from the legend of King Arthur.

Two years before, Kent had designed another folly, the Hermitage. Although that did not house a real-life hermit, this one did have a human inhabitant – Stephen Duck, a rustic poet from Wiltshire who achieved fame as the Thresher Poet. He lived here with his wife and acted the part of Merlin for visitors.

The poet was a favourite of Caroline's, and at one time was put in charge of Duck Island in St James's Park. After Caroline's death, Duck took holy orders and became

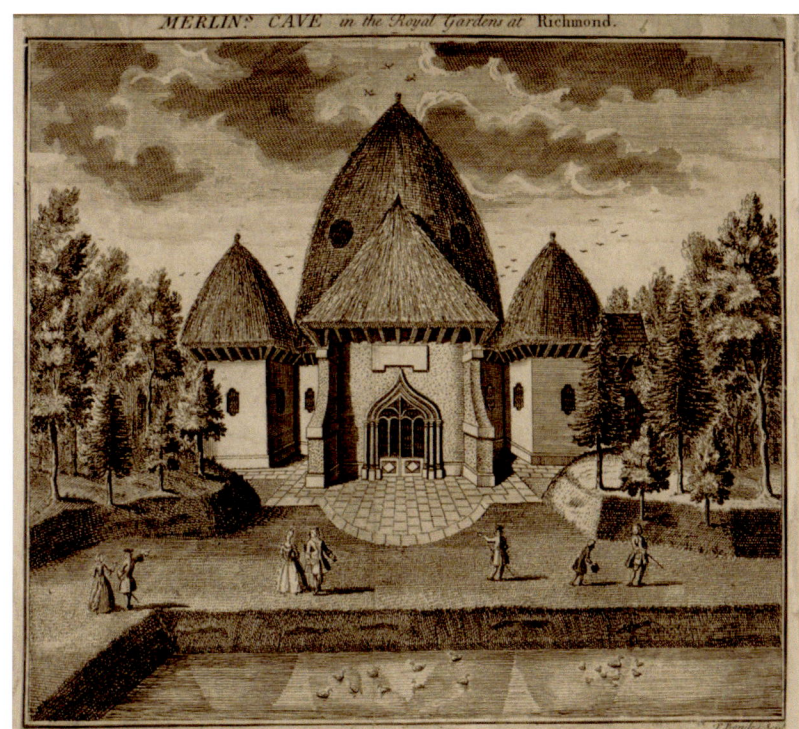

Merlin's Cave, one of the follies created by William Kent.

a popular preacher at Kew, before being appointed vicar at Byfleet. He met a sad end, drowned in the Thames in 1756. Both follies were later demolished, Merlin's Cave being sold for scrap.

Monument, The

There is a curious story behind the granite column on the pavement outside Brentford County Court. Known as The Monument, it was created in 1909 from two pillars that once supported lamps on the former bridge taking the High Street over the Grand Union Canal. It commemorates major events in Brentford's history.

The idea for creating it came from a local antiquary, Sir Montagu Sharpe, author of *Middlesex in British, Roman and Saxon Times*, and who was keen to promote the town's place – perhaps generally overlooked – in English history.

The Monument first stood on a wharf at the foot of Ferry Lane, where it gradually became buried under piles of coal unloaded from barges there, until it was forgotten. It was rediscovered in 1955 and moved, first further along Ferry Lane, then – in 1992 – to its present position at the junction of Brentford High Street and Alexandra Road.

The Monument commemorates Julius Caesar's crossing of the Thames, in 54 BC; King Offa's council of Brentford, in 781; King Canute's defeat by King Edmund Ironside at the first Battle of Brentford, in 1016; and the second Battle of Brentford,

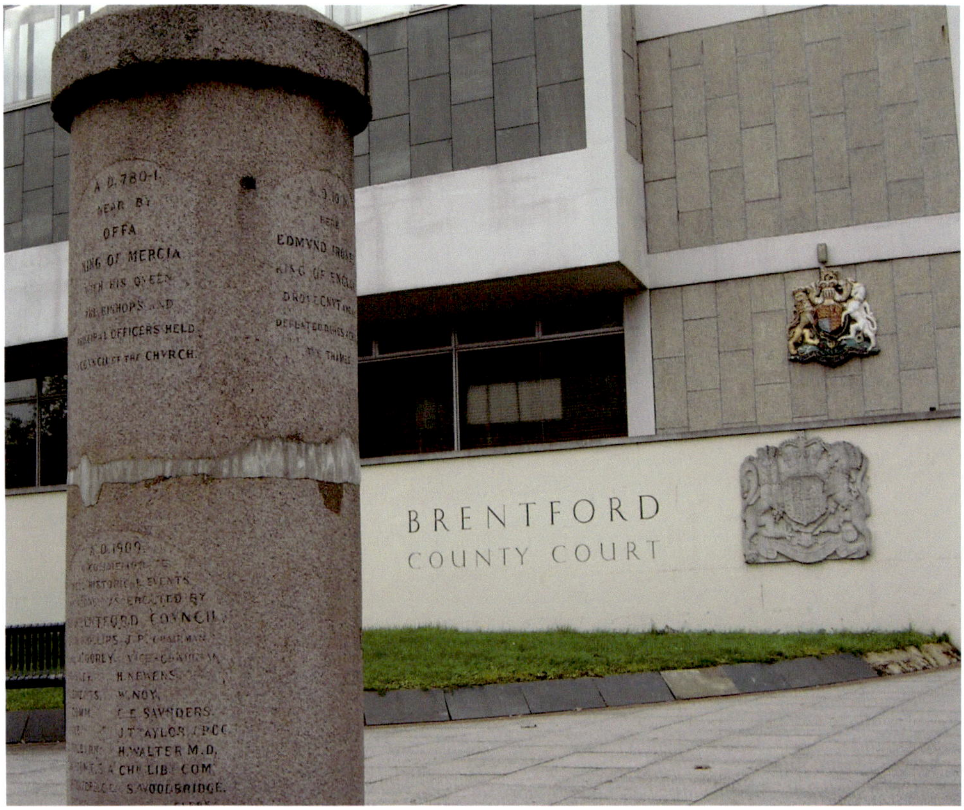

A–Z of Kew and Brentford

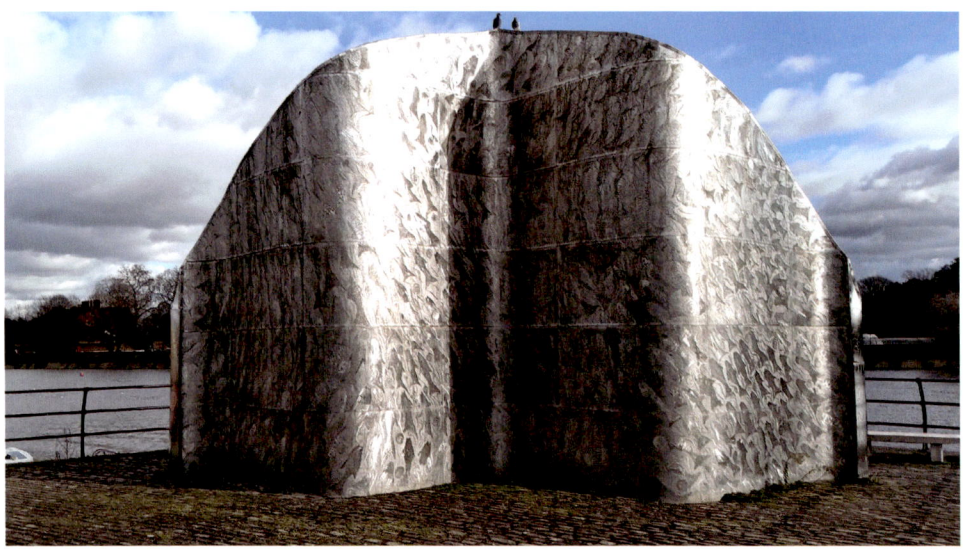

The Monument, recording key events in Brentford's past. (Kt0208 under Creative Commons)

A sculpture called *Liquidity* stands on the original site of Brentford's Monument. (Andy Scott and Kt0288 under Creative Commons)

fought between Royalists and Parliamentarians, in 1642. A plaque at the foot of the column reads:

> This historic memorial was moved to this site in November 1992 by the London Borough of Hounslow to commemorate the 350th anniversary of the English Civil War and the Battle of Brentford which took place on and around this site on 12 November 1642.

The badly deteriorated inscriptions were re-lettered in black in 2017, by which time a new monument had been placed at the original site. A grand stainless steel sculpture etched with images of local wildlife, named *Liquidity*, was unveiled in 1909 by the Duke of Northumberland.

Musical Museum, The

Creating musical instruments that play automatically might sound like something from the modern age, but the Musical Museum in Brentford demonstrates that, for

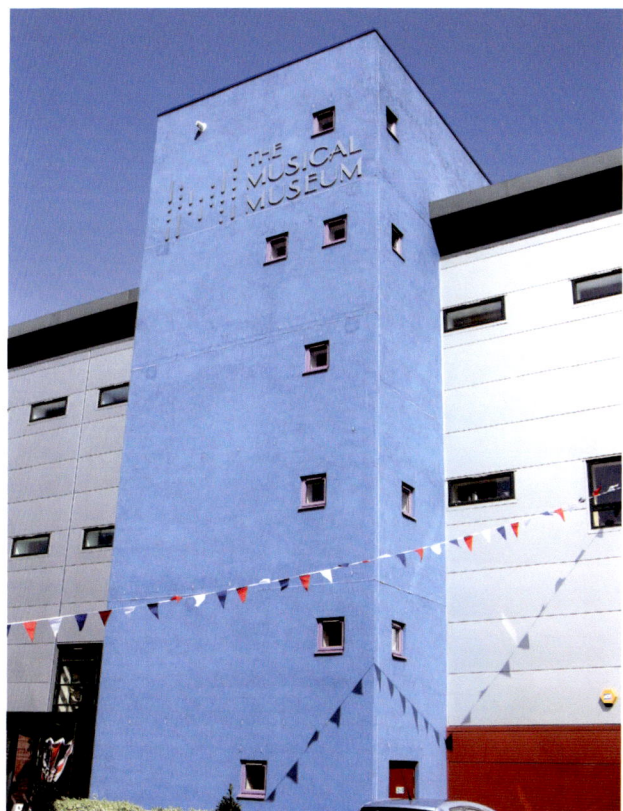

The Musical Museum.
(Jim Linwood Seeburg under Creative Commons)

400 years, madcap inventors have been creating machines that can be programmed to do just that.

The museum was opened in 1963 in the disused St George's Church at No. 368 Brentford High Street, moving a few doors down into purpose-built premises at No. 399 in 2008.

It was formed from a small collection of automated pianos built up by an enthusiast called Frank Holland. Looking for a home for them he approached the church authorities and was allowed to use the space, and was appointed caretaker. Gillian Clegg writes in *Brentford Past*:

> Holland, wearing a velvet smoking cap complete with tassel, was famous for the idiosyncratic afternoon tours he gave the public. He likened his collection to a zoo full of rare and exotic animals, all with their different colours and cries ... In 1966 the collection's scope was extended to include the history of the piano and the development of all kinds of automatic instruments – street organs, musical boxes, nickelodeons, barrel organs.

Today the museum has a large performance space on the first floor where gigs are held, and a Wurlitzer Pipe Organ, originally housed in the Regal Cinema, Kingston upon Thames, on which resident organist Richard Hills gives recitals.

National Archives

Kew's second world-famous institution, after the Royal Botanic Gardens, is the National Archives, formerly known as the Public Records Office, which holds priceless documents and a wealth of data on every aspect of England, Wales and its people. Scotland and Northern Ireland have their own archives.

All our history is documented here, in 11,000,000 files covering the past 1,000 years, housed on 115 miles of shelving, in a building built in 1977 on the site of a First World War hospital.

Below and overleaf: The National Archives, Kew, and the Magna Carta, one of its treasures. (National Archives)

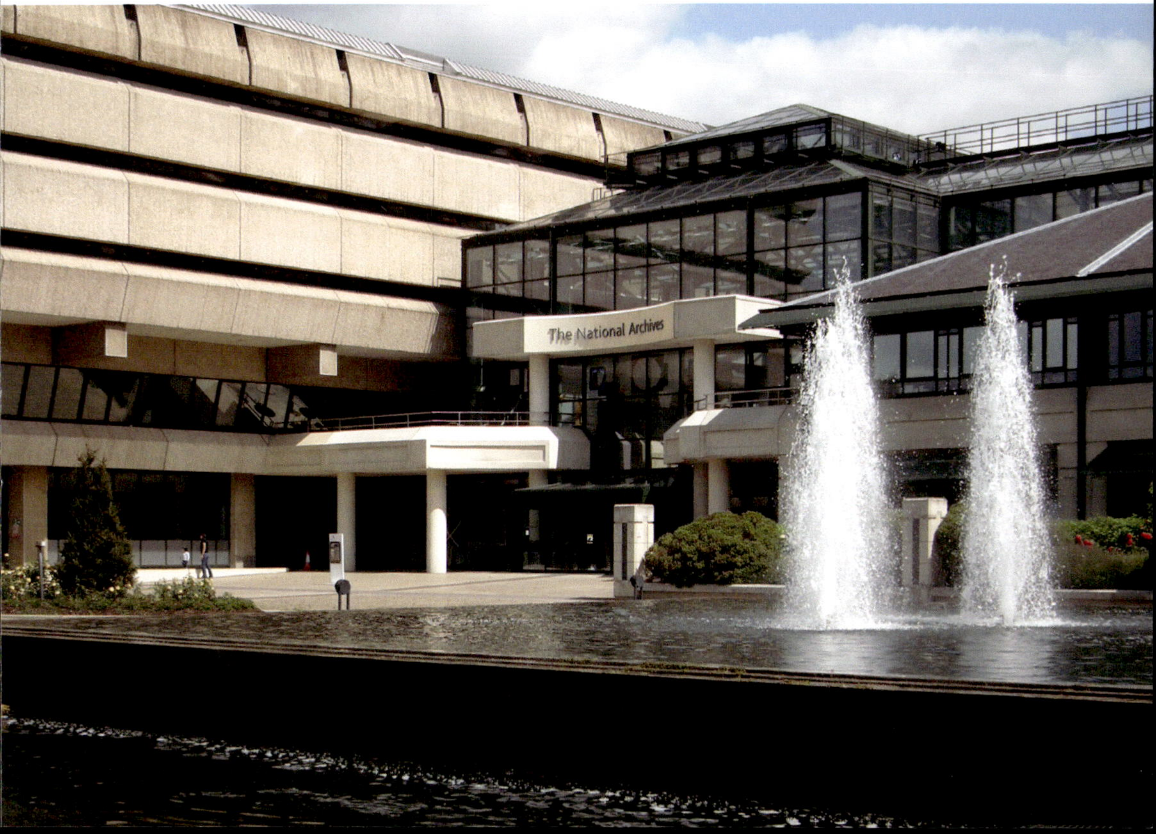

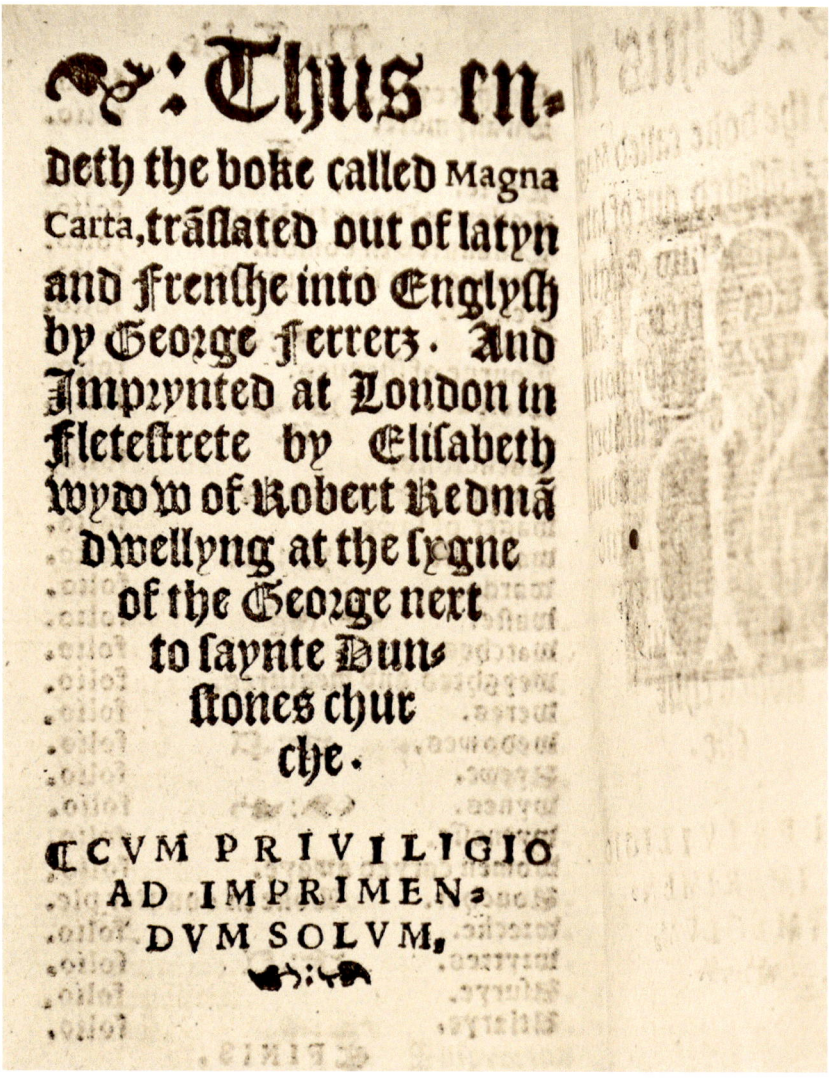

Among the treasures to be found here – the original documents open to study by anyone over the age of sixteen – are the Domesday Book, the audit of William the Conqueror's newly acquired kingdom, which dates from 1086; Magna Carta, the 1215 charter which established that the monarch and their government were not above the law; a note from Geoffrey Chaucer, author of *The Canterbury Tales*, requesting time off his work as controller of the London Wool Quay; the treatment of the Windrush Generation, immigrants from the Caribbean who came to Britain in the 1950s; scandals such as the Profumo affair and the defection of the spy Kim Philby; and many more.

Every aspect of public life is covered, including most government documents that are over thirty years old, armed forces service records, court cases, land ownership, census records, bomb damage during wartime, and registers of doctors and nurses.

Observatory, Kew

George III was fascinated by science, and when he established his principal retreat, to be called Richmond Palace, in 1760 in what is now known as Old Deer Park, an observatory was attached to it.

Observing the heavens had become hugely fashionable among those wealthy enough to own sufficiently powerful telescopes. George was keen that The King's Observatory be completed before the transit of Venus across the sun, which was to occur on 3 June 1769. This was to be a hugely significant event, enabling astronomers to calculate with greater accuracy the size of the solar system, and the distance between the earth and sun. A few years later, the observatory was the scene of another great scientific advance. It was used to successfully test a marine chronometer, designed by John Harrison, that enabled mariners to calculate their longitude at sea.

The Palladian observatory, surmounted by a cupola to hold the telescope, was the only part of the palace to be built. It passed out of royal hands in 1840 and, renamed Kew Observatory, was administered by first the British Association for the Advancement of Science, then the Royal Society, and finally the Meteorological Office.

Below left and below right: The King's Observatory, Kew, and the transit of Venus, once viewed through its telescope. (Andy Scott and Benutzer-Klingon under Creative Commons)

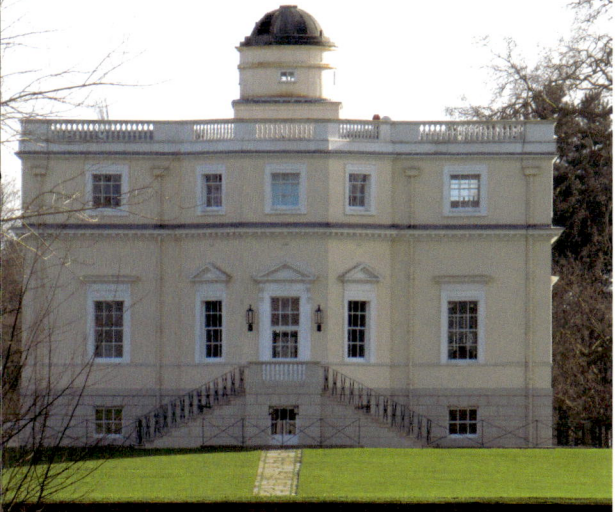
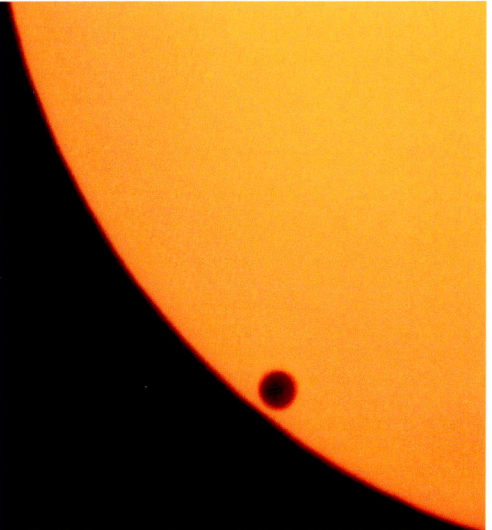

In the mid-nineteenth century it was an important centre for research into the sun and its influences on the earth, geomagnetism and meteorology.

It was the Met Office's main observatory, at which experiments were made in using automatic instruments to record the weather, and essential, systematic records were kept of key meteorological phenomena including temperature, atmospheric pressure and humidity.

The Met Office moved out in 1980 and the building was converted into offices, reverting to its original name of The King's Observatory. It became a private house in 2014, and occasional tours are available.

Oliver's Ait

There is a local legend attached to the name of this small island lying in the River Thames between Kew's rail and road bridges. It is that 'Oliver' refers to Cromwell, who fought a fierce battle at Brentford during the English Civil War. Before that time it was known as Strand Ayt, and is also known today as Oliver's Island. As David Blomfield writes in *Kew Past*:

> Oliver Cromwell either withdrew here briefly to discuss his military plans or escaped there from the Bull's Head on the north bank via an underground passageway. Historians are sceptical, but signs of what might have been steps were found when the pub was recently rebuilt – and why otherwise should the ait have got its name?

A second small island, Brentford Ait, in the river between Kew Gardens and Watermans Park is now a bird sanctuary. It was notorious in the eighteenth century for the Three Swans pub, where royals and the rich conducted liaisons with their lovers.

One Over the Ait is not an island at all but a modern pub just upriver of Kew Bridge, popular with fans of Brentford Football Club.

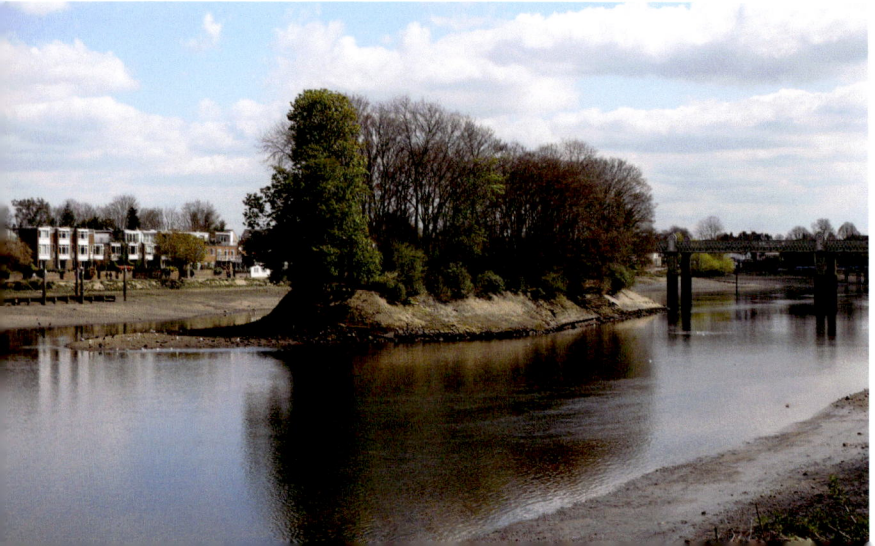

Oliver's Ait, or Island, may be named after Cromwell. (Ethan Doyle White under Creative Commons)

P

Palm House, The

The Palm House is the most splendid building in Kew Gardens; a beautiful creation in wrought iron and glass. It was completed in 1848 and was the first major structure built from these materials.

The architect was Decimus Burton. It is an elegant building, housing an indoor rainforest and living laboratory, enabling Kew's scientists to research the medicinal benefits of plants.

Here, rubber trees, oil palms and cocoa trees thrive, among a collection that includes many endangered species, some extinct in their natural habitats. It is also home to

Below and overleaf: The Palm House creates ideal conditions for plants that thrive in the rainforest. (Patchez99 and Peter Clarke under Creative Commons)

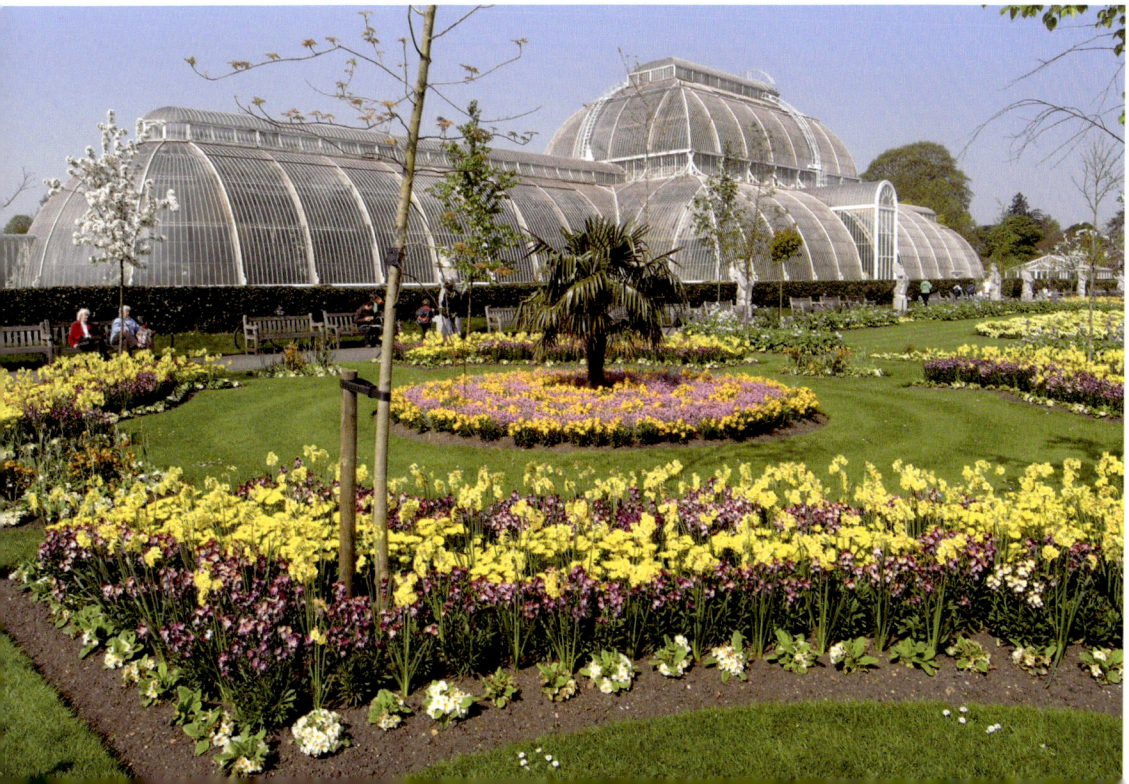

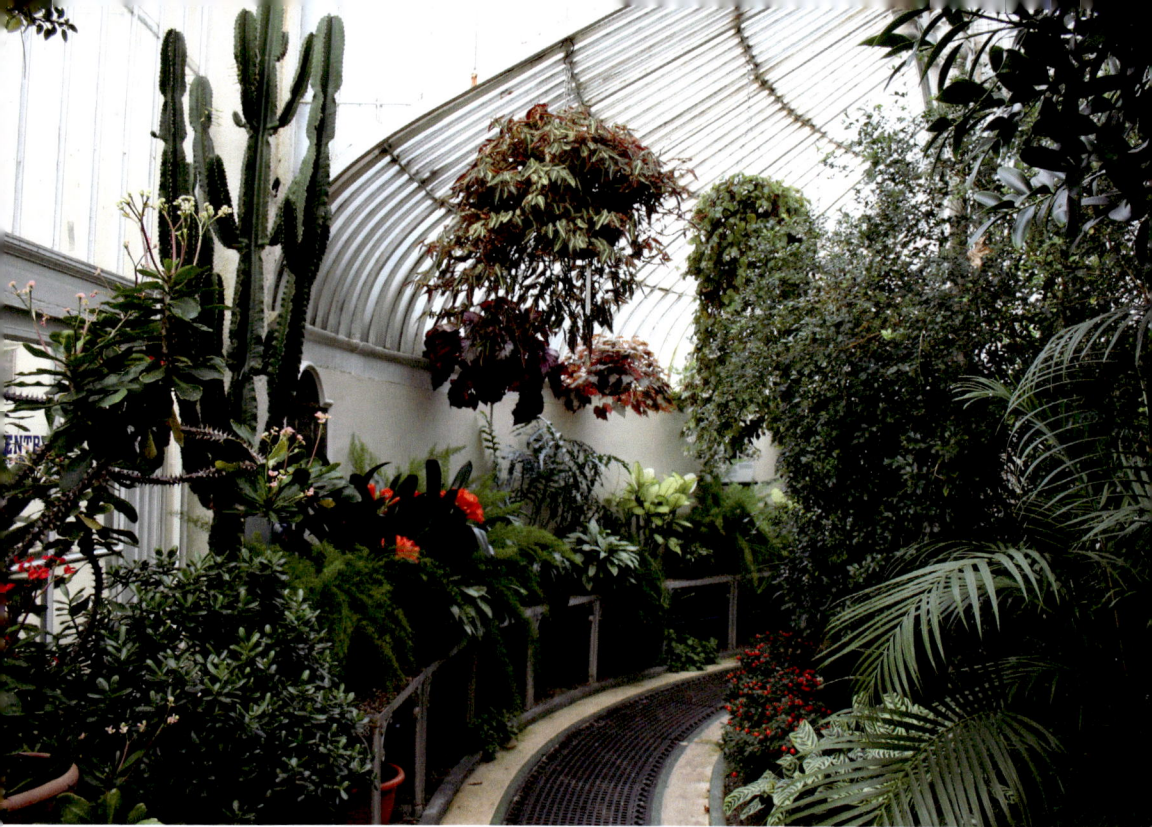

the oldest pot plant in the world, an *Encephalartos altensteinii*, a palm-like plant from South Africa brought into the Palm House when it was opened.

Great practical ingenuity was demonstrated in the design of the building, which when first opened had to be heated using coke. Boilers were hidden beneath it, and fuel brought to them along underground railways, the carts pushed by hand. Ingeniously, the tunnels also took smoke away to a chimney disguised as an Italianate bell tower.

People Just Do Nothing

The runaway success of the BBC comedy show *People Just Do Nothing* has put some unlikely Brentford locations on the tourist map. The show, which ran for five series from 2014, was set and largely filmed in and around the Haverfield Estate, where a line of tower blocks stand out in stark contrast to the suburb they rise from.

The show is about a pirate radio station called Kurupt FM, which broadcasts illegally from one of those towers. It follows the lives of MC Grindah (played by Allan Mustafa) and DJ Beats (Hugo Chegwin). Mustafa and Chegwin created the comedy, along with its other main performers, Steve Stamp and Asim Chaudhry.

Brit Movie Tours offers a walking tour of fifteen locations that feature regularly in the show, including Brentford railway station, Green Dragon Lane, Brentford County Court, McDonald's and the Weir pub.

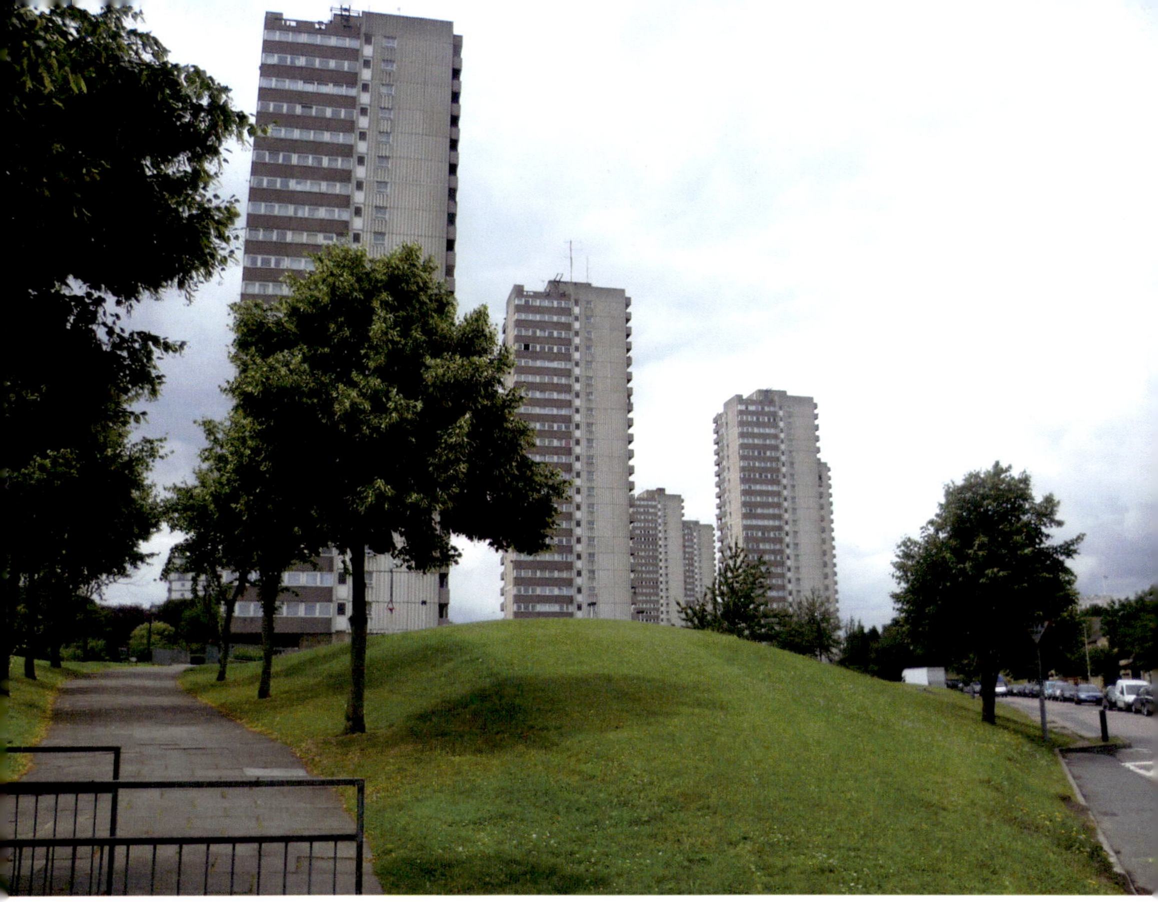

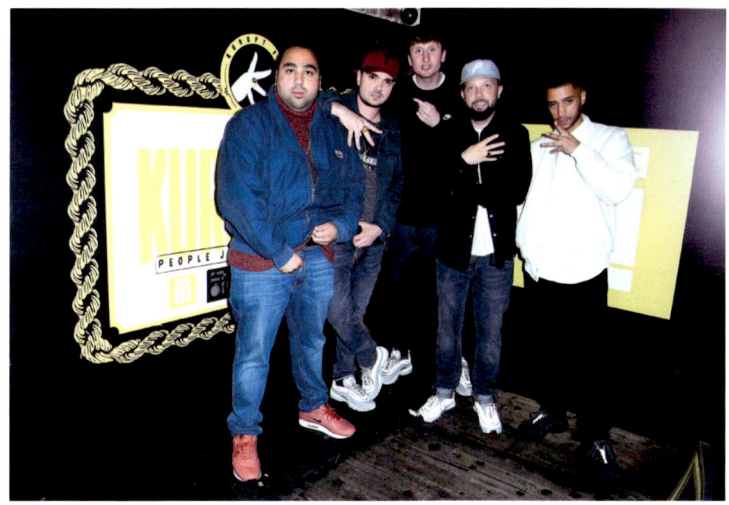

Above: *People Just Do Nothing* is set in the tower blocks of the Haverfield Estate, Brentford. (Marathon under Creative Commons)

Right: *People Just Do Nothing* cast members, from left: Asim Chaudhry, Allan Mustafa, Steve Stamp, Hugo Chegwin and Daniel Sylvester Woolford. (Alamy)

Chegwin and Stamp grew up on the Haverfield Estate as next-door neighbours and, while the show is set there, some episodes were filmed in Acton and Peckham.

People Just Do Nothing has received eight Bafta nominations and four wins, and spawned the movie spin-off *Big in Japan*. The stars had a show on Radio 1X and have appeared in character at a string of clubs and festivals across Europe.

Pocahontas

Pocahontas was a North American, First Nation princess who is hugely famous thanks to the Disney film about her. Much less well known is that she married an Englishman and lived for a time in Brentford, making her almost certainly the town's most exotic former resident.

She was the daughter of Powhatan, a powerful tribal leader and, as Gillian Clegg records in *Brentford Past*, 'is credited with helping to maintain peace between the Indians and the colonists of the first permanent English settlement in North America, at Jamestown, Virginia'.

As a young girl, Pocahontas (c. 1595–1617) is said to have saved the life of John Smith, the founder of the colony, by pleading for his life when her father wanted him killed.

In 1609, when relations had once again broken down, she was kidnapped by the settlers and held hostage, finally being returned in exchange for seven English prisoners. While in captivity she converted to Christianity, took the name Rebecca, and met John Rolfe. They married in 1614, a union that brought peace to Virginia for a number of years.

In 1616 the couple sailed to England, where Pocahontas was greeted as a celebrity, and received at Court. Sadly, she fell ill and came to Brentford, staying at a house in

Below left: Pocahontas's statue in Gravesend, where she died. (Matt Statter under Creative Commons)

Below right: A plaque near the place where Pocahontas lived in Brentford.

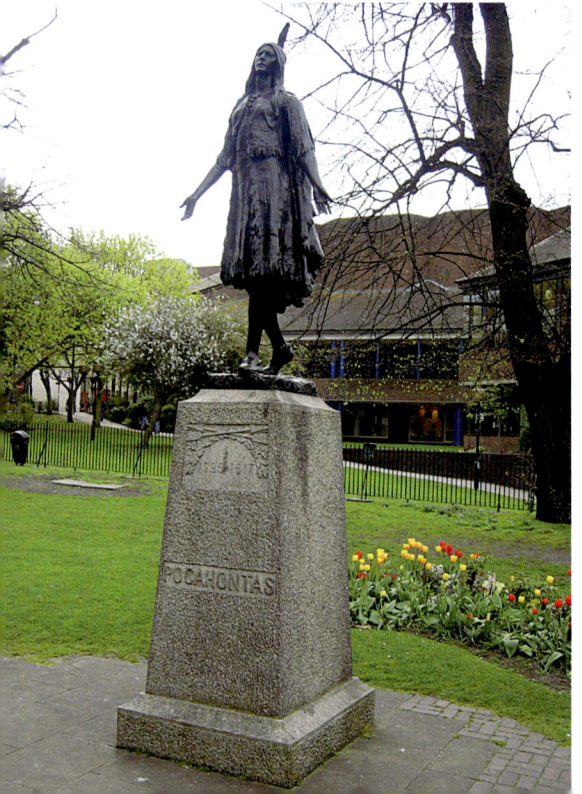 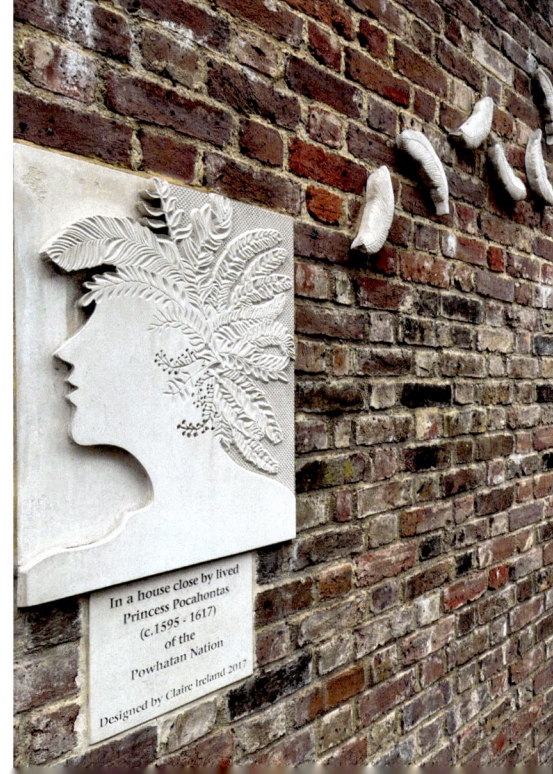

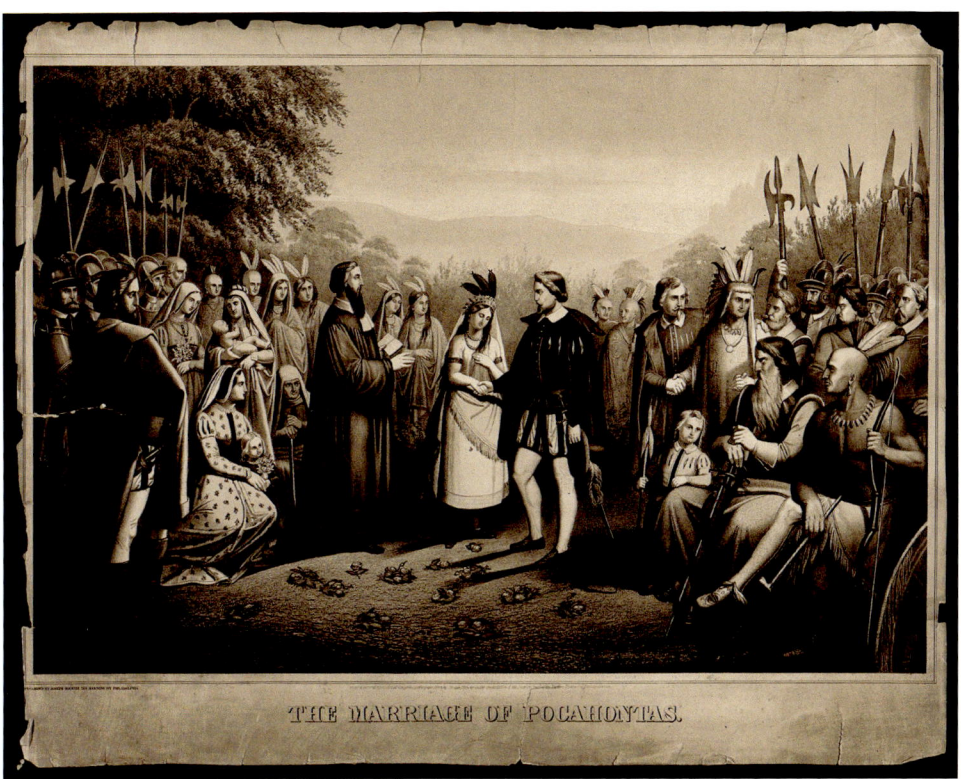

Pocahontas's marriage to John Rolfe. (Wellcome Collection)

London Road, near where the Royal Mail Delivery Office stands now, to recuperate. In the spring of 1617 the couple decided to return to America but, tragically, Pocahontas died on their ship as it passed Gravesend. A statue stands there in her honour.

Pope, Alexander

The poet (1688–1744) who gave us such phrases as 'damning with faint praise' and 'to err is human; to forgive, divine' wrote what are perhaps his most famous lines for Prince Frederick, son of George II. Pope gave the prince a dog to take on the walks he enjoyed from his home in Kew, and wrote this couplet for its collar:

> I am His Highness' dog at Kew;
> Pray tell me, sir, whose dog are you?

Queen Elizabeth I

Elizabeth I visited Kew in 1560 at the invitation of her favourite Robert Dudley, Earl of Leicester, who owned Kew Park, land now part of the Royal Botanic Gardens. She had given him the property in 1558 and, two years later, he invited her to his new home for a banquet.

No expense was spared on a meal at which the meat from ten sheep, six lambs, six herons, forty-eight teal, the same number of quail, fifty-six pigeons, twenty capon (castrated cockerels), 600 eggs, forty-one loaves and 86 lbs of butter were consumed.

The puddings included what may have been the first pineapples to be grown in England. The bill of £83 16s 6d equates to £35,000 today, according to the Bank of England's Inflation Calculator.

Elizabeth lived for part of the year at Richmond Palace, a few miles to the south, and would ride to meet Dudley beneath an elm on the banks of the Thames, a point known afterwards as Queen Elizabeth's Lawn. The spot is now beneath Kew Gardens' car park. The elm, which fell during a storm in the nineteenth century, was made into a kitchen table for Queen Victoria, and taken to her home, Osborne House, on the Isle of Wight.

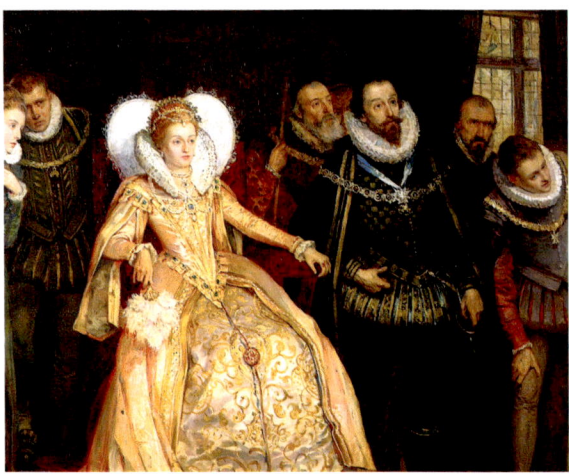 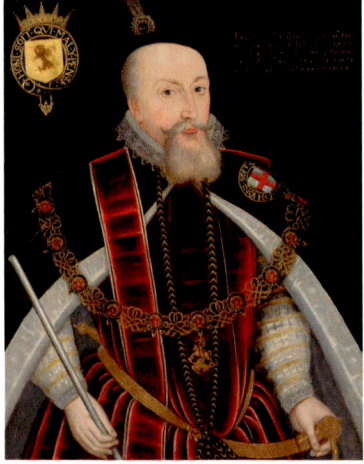

Above left and above right: Elizabeth I and her favourite, Robert Dudley. (Wellcome Collection and Yale Center for British Art)

Rankin, Robert

Brentford is the setting for a series of novels described by their author, Robert Rankin, as 'a mix of science fiction, fantasy, the occult, urban legends, running gags, metafiction, steampunk and outrageous characters'. He also describes it as 'far-fetched fiction'.

His *Brentford Trilogy*, which actually stretches to eleven novels, includes *The Brentford Triangle* (1982) about the thwarting of an alien invasion, and *The Brentford Chainstore Massacre* (1997) about an attempt to clone Jesus from the Turin Shroud.

Recurring characters include John Vincent Omally and Jim Pooley – respectively an Irishman living in Brentford and his best friend, who are the heroes of the series; Neville, barman at the fictional Flying Swan pub; and a Brentford shopkeeper who shares a name with the late royal dress designer Norman Hartnell. Norman has invented a device that can transport the Great Pyramid from Egypt to Brentford.

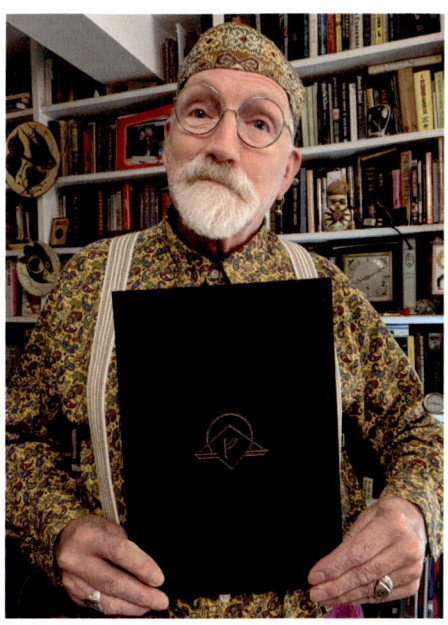

Robert Rankin, author of *The Brentford Triangle*. (Dr John C. Bullas under Creative Commons)

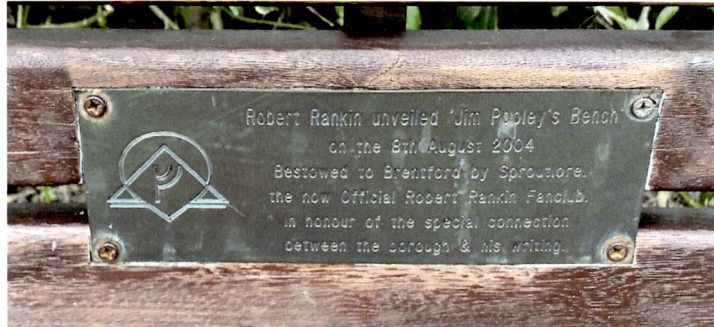

Left and below: Jim Pooley's bench, named after Rankin's character, at Brentford Library. (Andy Scott and West London Dweller under Creative Commons)

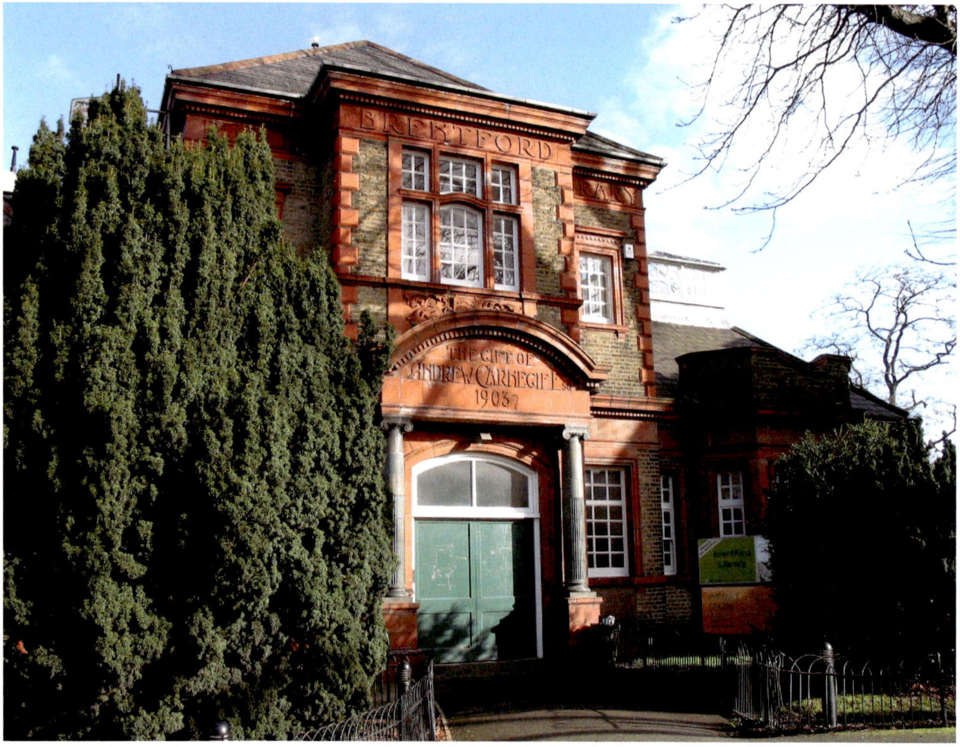

A seat bearing a plaque naming it as 'Jim Pooley's Bench' was unveiled by Robert Rankin at Brentford Library in 2004. It honours 'the special connection with the borough and his writing'.

Rayon

Rayon, an artificial silk that was to revolutionise the textile industry, was invented in Kew. Charles Cross and Edward Bevan were a pair of Kew-based organic chemists who, in 1892, discovered cellulose xanthate, which they named Viscose.

As David Blomfield writes in *Kew Past*:

> At the time there was a business in South Avenue called Zurich Incandescent Light Works. Its manager, Charles Stearn, suggested that [light bulb] filaments could be made from this Viscose. The initial experiments were disappointing, but Cross and Stearn found that Viscose made good artificial silk, and set up the Viscose Spinning Syndicate in Station Avenue.

Viscose was a major advance in the production of synthetic textiles, but production never took pace in Kew. Rather, Cross and Stearn sold their company to Courtaulds, the world's leading producer of man-made fibre, who produced it in Coventry.

Red Barn Murder, The

One of the most notorious nineteenth-century murderers was finally captured in Brentford. William Corder had arranged to meet his lover, Maria Marten, and elope with her. Instead, he shot her dead. The story was dramatised as *The Red Barn Murder*, a hugely popular melodrama.

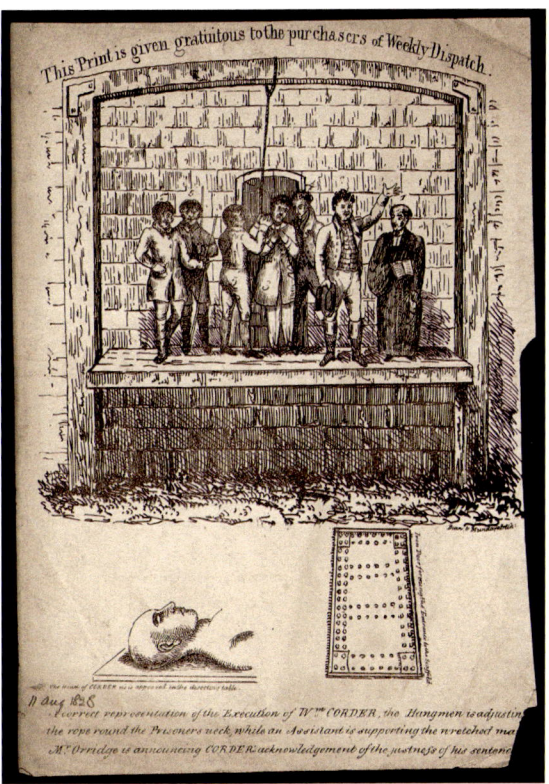

The hanging of the Red Barn murderer William Corder, arrested in Brentford. (Wellcome Collection)

Following the killing, in 1827 in the Red Barn, a local landmark in the village of Polstead, Essex, Corder wrote letters to Maria's family claiming she was well but, a year later, her body was discovered in a shallow grave beside the barn. Corder was traced to Brentford, where he had married. He was sent for trial in Bury St Edmunds, Suffolk, and hanged before a baying crowd.

The story provoked huge public interest, ghoulish tourists flocked to the murder site, and many articles, several songs and other plays were written about it.

Corder was tracked down at Everley Grove, a boarding house for ladies, in Ealing Lane, Brentford, which he was running with his new wife, Mary Moore. He was clearly something of a ladies' man. Mary Moore was one of 100 women who had responded to a lonely-hearts advertisement he placed in *The Times*.

When Corder's rooms at the boarding house were searched, two pistols bought on the day of the murder were found, along with a French passport, suggesting he intended to flee if alerted that the police were closing in.

The novelist Thomas Hardy read of the arrest in the *Dorset County Chronicle* and noted in his diary that Corder was apprehended 'in parlour with four ladies at breakfast, in dressing gown & had a watch before him by which he was "minuting" the boiling of some eggs'.

Regeneration

Brentford has been in a process of transformation since the 1980s, a regeneration that has gathered pace in the twenty-first century. While Kew – Brentford's middle-class cousin across the river – has long been confident of its own identity as an upmarket suburb with a village feel, Brentford has been undergoing the sometimes painful process of transition. It is morphing from a run-down and neglected post-industrial area into a vibrant riverside community where creative industries can thrive, thanks to a multi-billion-pound regeneration scheme.

Steadily, the wharves and industrial buildings that filled the strip of land between the Thames and the High Street have been replaced with apartment blocks, shops, restaurants and riverside spaces.

The Brentford Town Centre Regeneration Project, run by Hounslow Council, recognises that 'The meeting point of River Thames, River Brent and the Grand Union Canal provides a unique historical and environmental setting to the town centre' and intends to develop the area while recognising its industrial and waterways heritage.

One of the biggest elements is the Brentford Riverside Project, from developers Ballymore, under which almost 900 homes are being built on a 12-acre site between the High Street and River Brent. The development will include new shops, a supermarket, gym, leisure centre, and an arts centre and cinema.

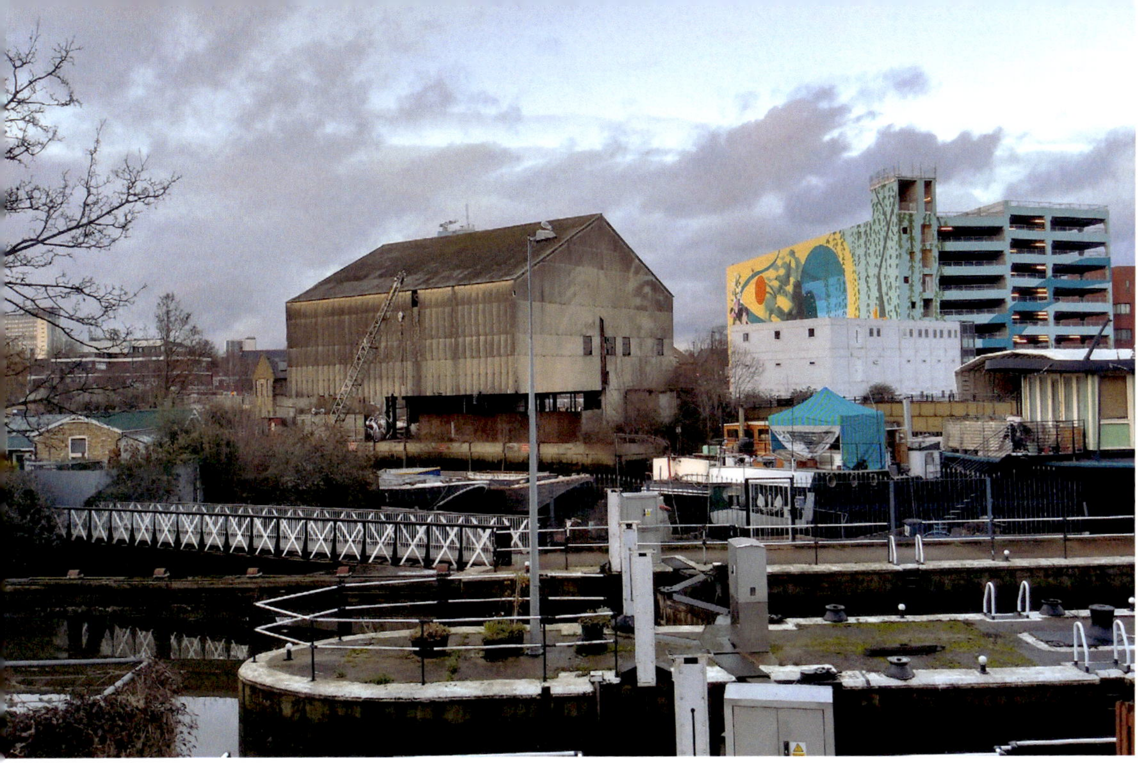

Above and below: Regeneration underway in Brentford. (Andy Scott under Creative Commons)

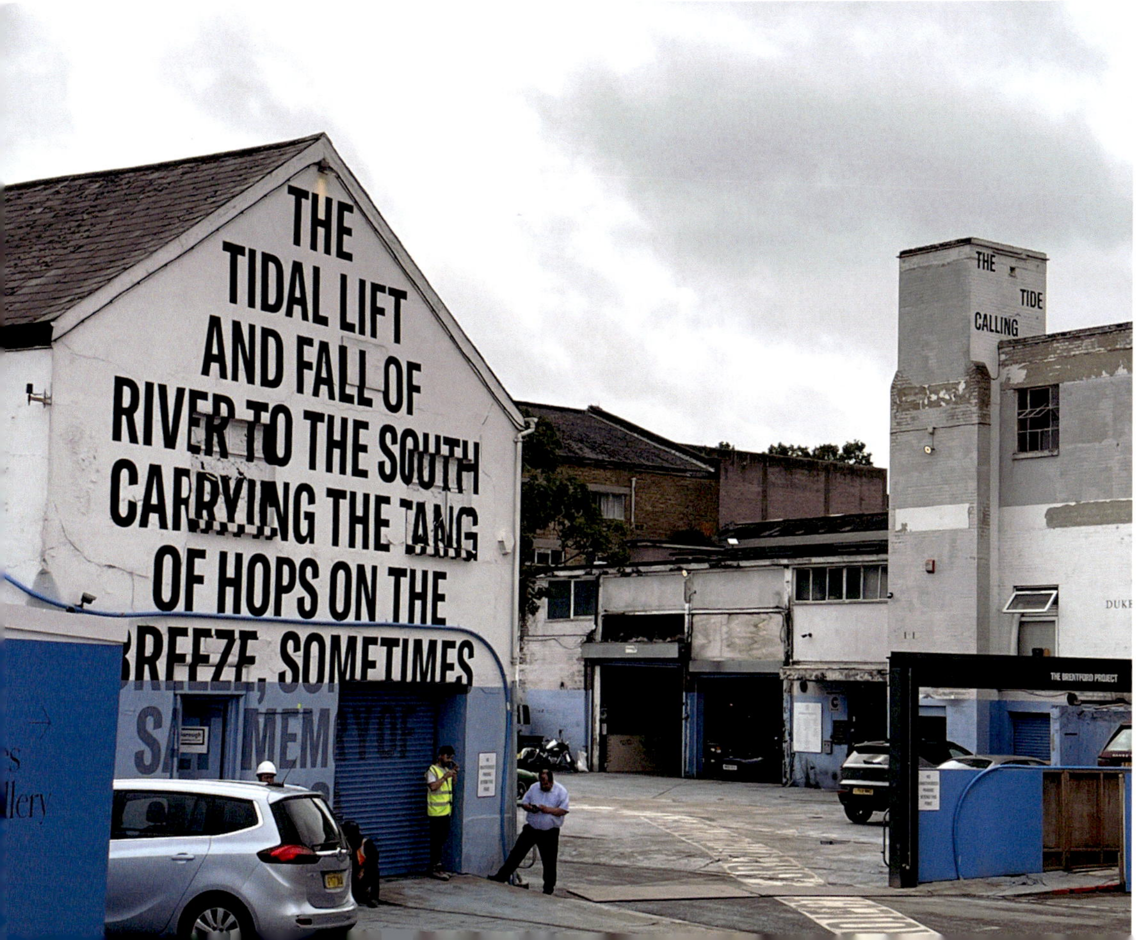

Shakespeare, William

Brentford plays a walk-on role in William Shakespeare's *The Merry Wives of Windsor*, and the author had a connection with the Three Pigeons, an inn that stood in Brentford's Market Place.

At one stage the play's plot requires Falstaff to find a disguise, and the character Mrs Ford suggests one: 'My maid's aunt, the fat woman of Brentford, has a gown above.' But Mrs Ford is setting Falstaff up. In a later line she says: 'I would my husband would meet him in this shape: he cannot abide the old woman of Brentford; he swears she's a witch; forbade her my house and hath threatened to beat her.'

In *The Lodger: Shakespeare on Silver Street*, Charles Nicholls explains the playwright's connection to Brentford, and the Three Pigeons:

> It was owned by a colleague in the King's Men, John Lowin. Lowin acted alongside Shakespeare [in 1603 and 1604] ... He is listed in the First Folio, as one of the 'principal actors' in Shakespeare's plays ... It is not known when Lowin became owner of the Three Pigeons. Another of Shakespeare's colleagues, Augustine Phillips, owned a house at nearby Mortlake, just across the river on the south bank. This house seems

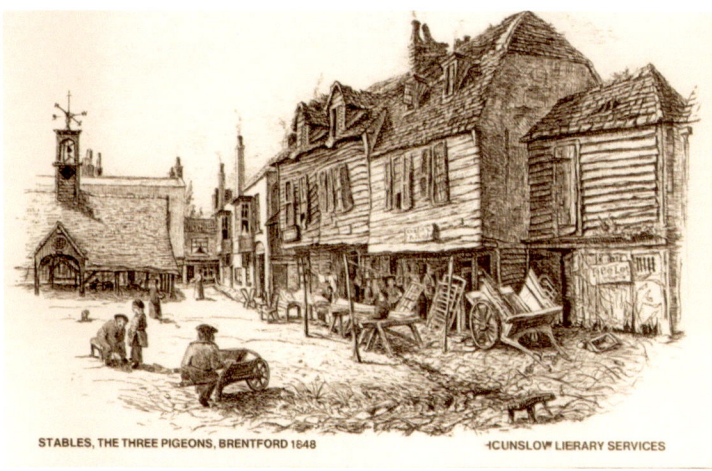

The Three Pigeons, a Brentford pub with a Shakespeare connection. (Hounslow Library Services)

S

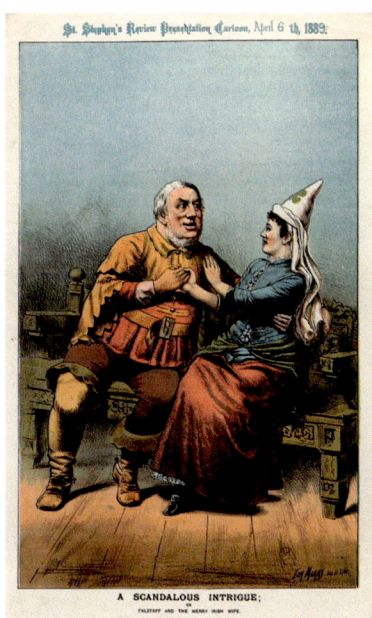

Sir William Harcourt as Falstaff in *The Merry Wives of Windsor*. (Wellcome Collection)

to have served as a base for the company in the summer of 1603, when the plague was at its height in the city. It is quite likely Shakespeare knew the Three Pigeons.

In another Brentford connection, Shakespeare's former landlord, Christopher Mountjoy, also had a house in the town.

Shakespeare (1564–1616) is not the only author of the period to write about Brentford. Charles Nicholl reveals that Brentford was generally well known in Shakespeare's time as a place of debauchery: a bacchanalian retreat for Londoners keen to let off steam, and loosen clothing.

Nicholl writes of Brentford in those days:

It sounds a pleasant, faintly pastoral escape from the [London] world of pimps and courtesans and sexual predation – but it is not ... in Shakespeare's time Brentford had a lurid reputation. It was 'a place of resort' for Londoners and had numerous prostitutes. It is alluded to in various plays and pamphlets of the period, almost invariably as a place for a dirty night or weekend.

In Thomas Dekker and John Webster's *Westward Ho!*, written in 1605–6, three lecherous men consider their options for a 'merry midsummer night' on the razzle with three wives of others and, out of a list of options – Ham, Blackwall, Limehouse – settle on Brentford, then known as Brainford, because 'There you are out of eyes, out of ears: private rooms, sweet linen, winking attendance, and what cheer you will!'

In Thomas Middleton and Thomas Dekker's *Roaring Girl* (1612) Brentford is chosen over Staines and Ware for 'a lecherous voyage'. In the final act of Ben Jonson's

The Alchemist (1610), Dr Subtle tries to get his girlfriend, Doll Common, to run away with him to Brentford, enticing her with: 'My bird of the night, we'll tickle it at the [Three] Pigeons.'

Nicholl comments:

> These are the typical connotations of Brentford – a place of amorous truancy, an escape into illicit pleasure; a place where no questions are asked, because everyone else is up to much the same thing, and where suitable accommodation is ready and waiting – private rooms, scented linen and ... discreet service ... Thus one went to make merry at Brainford.

The Three Pigeons, which dated from 1436 and went under various names during different periods of its long history, was severely damaged by fire in the 1920s, after which it became offices, and was demolished in 1950.

Smith's Crisps

To crisp eaters of a certain vintage, a little blue-paper twist of salt was an essential ingredient to their favourite snack. That groundbreaking blue package, created because – at the time – adding salt directly to crisps would cause them to go soggy in their greaseproof paper bags – made Smith's Crisps famous.

Such an innovative company needed a headquarters that reflected its modernity, and in 1927 built an art deco factory on the Golden Mile, a stretch of the Great West Road in Brentford. However, it wasn't founded there. Smith's Potato Crisps Ltd

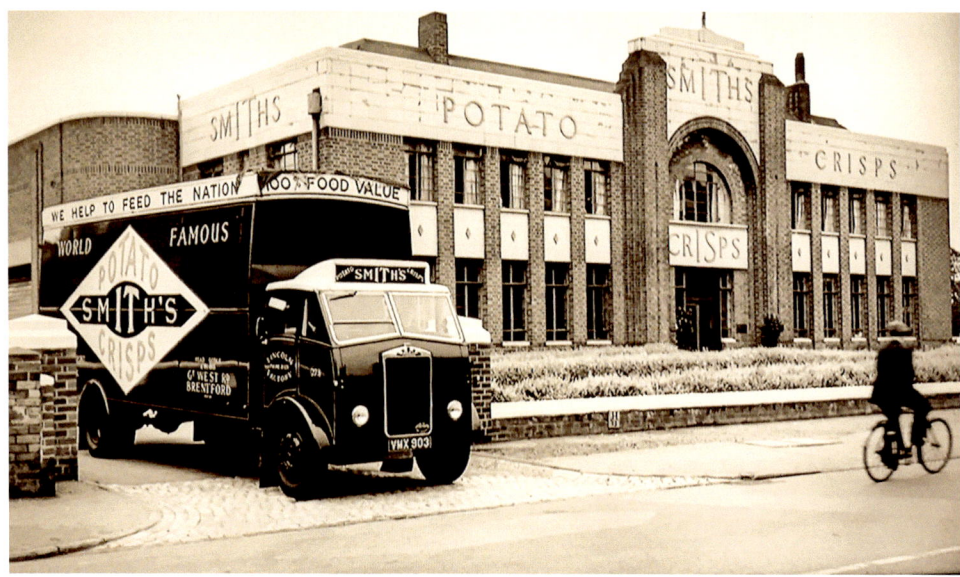

S

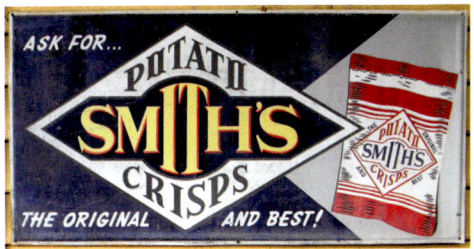
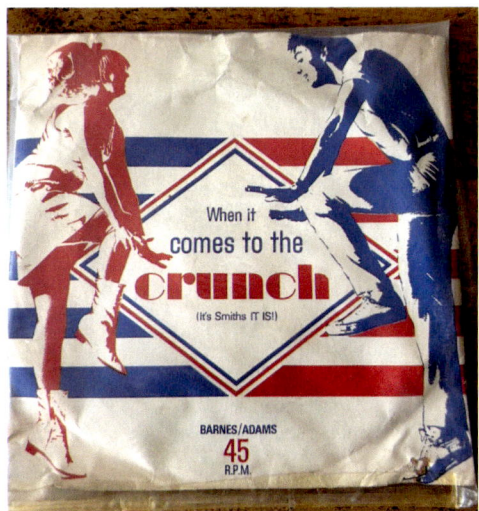

Opposite, above and right: Smith's Crisps' Brentford factory, a traditional ad, and a 'Do the Crunch' record sleeve.

was launched in 1913 by Frank Smith, a manager at a Smithfield wholesale grocery business, and Jim Viney.

The firm Smith worked for did a small line in crisps but Frank, realising how popular they were to publicans, because they made drinkers thirsty, knew he could do better.

Their first factory was in Cricklewood, North London, but progress was slow until Frank invented the little blue sachet, after which they quickly expanded. Frank Smith bought his partner out and later moved to Brentford. Two years after arriving here, Smith's had seven factories around the country. By 1934, 95 per cent of the 200 million packets of crisps sold annually in Britain were made by Smith's and, in 1955, they were selling 10 million packs a week.

However, competition came in the shape of Golden Wonder, a rival Scottish company that introduced flavoured crisps: starting with cheese and onion. Smith's fought back with salt and vinegar. A twenty-year-long flavours war followed, with more and more exotic flavourings being created.

Smith's launched a massive advertising campaign with a young singer and musician called Phil Collins, who was born in Chiswick. Collins toured the country teaching people to do a dance called The Crunch, and later joined Genesis.

Further innovation followed, with the company introducing Monster Munch, aimed at children, in 1977.

The Brentford factory was closed in 1970, following a steep decline in profits after the company was sold to the American firm General Mills. It was demolished in 1988. In 1998 another American company, PepsiCo, bought the brand.

PepsiCo also owned Walkers crisps, and later withdrew the Smith's name, choosing instead to market Walkers crisps with a long-running campaign fronted by then England football captain Gary Lineker. Smith's brands such as Quavers were re-branded as Walkers.

St Anne's Church

St Anne's Church dates from 1714, when Queen Anne, as lady of the manor, responding to an appeal from local worthies, donated the land it is built on and contributed £100 towards the building costs. It is probably no coincidence that it was dedicated to St Anne. This, however, was not the grand building we see today. Rather, it was a modest red-brick chapel, part of the parish of Kingston.

The first curate, Thomas Fogg, proved to be a controversial figure. In 1717 the Bishop of Winchester received a petition, signed by the great and good of Kew, containing a list of complaints about his behaviour.

It was said that he kept the collection rather than distributing it among the poor; did not live in the village, merely lodging here on Saturday nights; didn't ring the bell for long enough before services, thereby giving insufficient time for the faithful to gather themselves and cross the green for communion; failed to catechise the children; and read the divine service in his boots and with his riding clothes beneath his surplice, suggesting a desire for a quick getaway once the service was over.

Sadly, Queen Anne never worshipped at the church she had contributed so much to, dying within weeks of its dedication. Later in the eighteenth century, with royalty making their summer homes in Kew, the village really needed a parish church rather than this modest chapel. In 1769 Kew became a parish and the chapel became a church, and enjoyed considerable further royal patronage.

George III paid for a first extension, and George IV donated an organ. A second extension, in 1805, added a south aisle for the use of the royal family. Thanks to William IV the church was extended again, in 1837, when pews for 200 more worshipers were added. William decreed that these should be free of pew rents, and donated £5,000 to cover the cost. A mausoleum was added in 1851, and a dome in 1884.

St Anne's Church, Kew Green. (Patchez99 under Creative Commons)

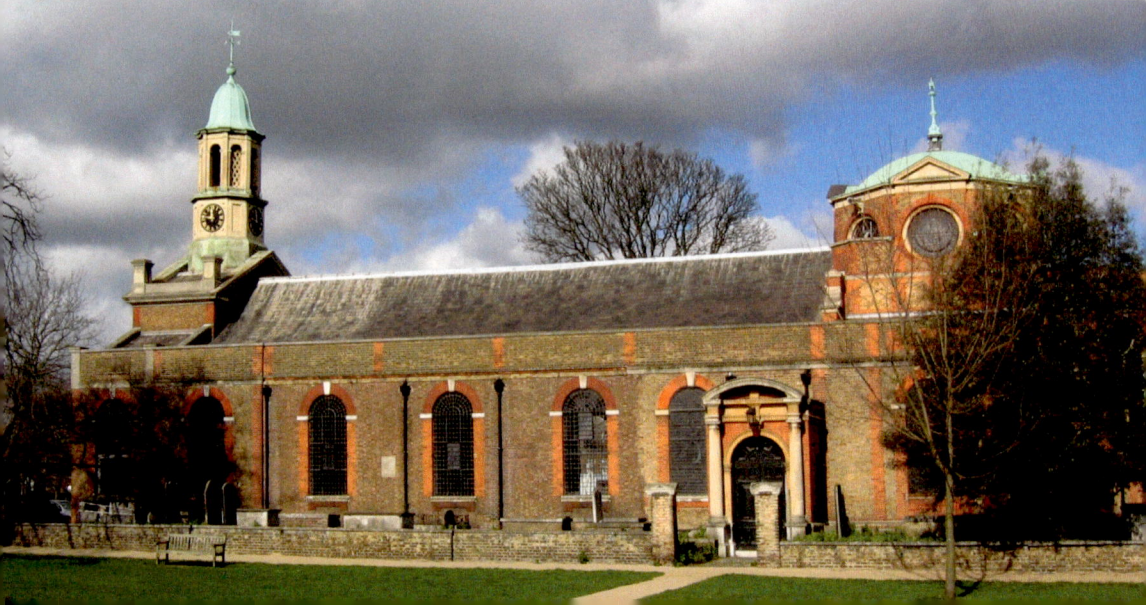

St Anne's played host to a royal wedding, in 1866, when Francis, Duke of Teck, married Princess Mary Adelaide of Cambridge, and a number of distinguished people are buried here.

Among them are several artists: the portrait and landscape painter Thomas Gainsborough, who died in 1788; George Engleheart (d. 1829), painter of portrait miniatures to George III; and Joshua Kirby, drawing master to the royal family (d. 1774). A number of distinguished botanists also rest here including: William Aiton (d. 1793), first keeper of the Royal Botanic Gardens; Sir William Hooker (d. 1865), director of the gardens; and his son, the botanist and explorer Sir Joseph Hooker (d. 1911).

St Lawrence's Church

The tower at St Lawrence's, in Brentford High Street, dates from 1480 and is the oldest structure in the town. The rest of the original building, established in 1175 when there was a chapel alongside the Hospital of St Lawrence, was lost when extensive rebuilding took place in 1762.

St Lawrence's Church, Brentford. (Jim Linwood under Creative Commons)

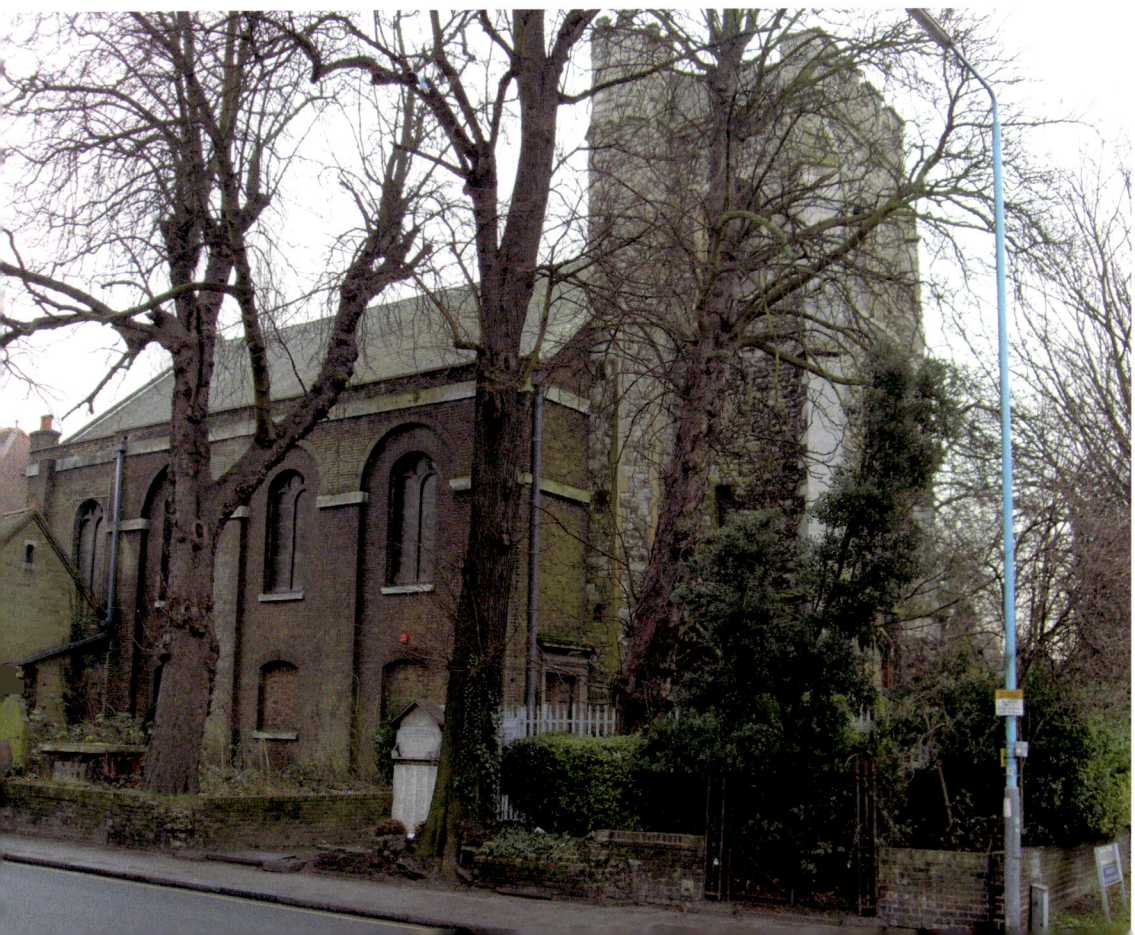

The church became redundant in 1961 when a number of Brentford parishes were amalgamated, and stood empty for decades. Numerous schemes to find a new use for it were mooted, but none came to fruition until 2020 when plans to build apartment blocks around the church were approved as part of the Brentford Project. The churchyard will become a park open to residents, and the church will, according to the developers, Ballymore, 'become a culinary and cultural hub for the community, and play host to pop-ups, events and shows'.

Steam Museum

The London Museum of Water and Steam, to give it its full title, started life as the Grand Junction Waterworks Company in 1837. Here, water from the Thames was

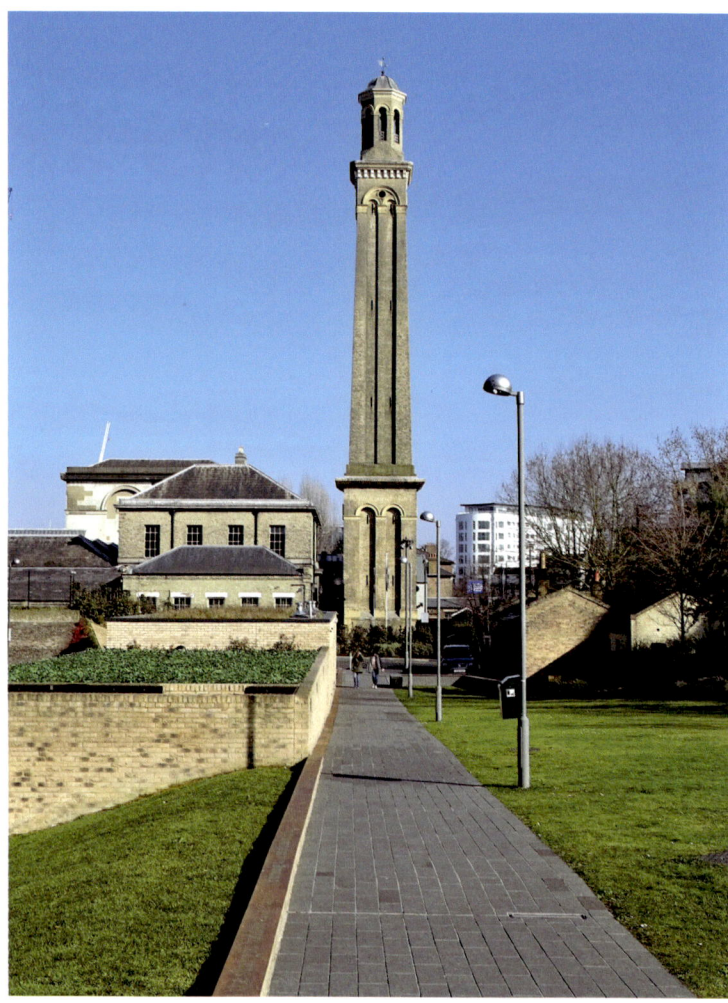

The London Museum of Water and Steam. (Neil Theasby under Creative Commons)

pumped into filter beds from which, now clean and suitable for drinking, it was pumped via a reservoir at Campden Hill to homes in Bayswater, Paddington and Kensington.

Charles Dickens visited in 1850 and wrote an account in his *Household Words* magazine:

> We were introduced to the great engine. What a monster! Imagine an enormous see-saw, with a steam engine at one end, and a pump at the other. Fancy this 'beam' some ten yards long, and 28 tons in weight, moving on a pivot in the middle, the end of which shows a circumference greater than the crown of the biggest hat ever worn. See, with what earnest deliberation the 'see' or engine, pulls up the 'saw' or balance box of the pump, which then comes down upon the watertrap with the ferocious aplomb of 49 tons, sending 400 gallons of water in one tremendous squirt nearly the twentieth part of a mile high; that is to the top of the stand-pipe.

The elegant brick campanile, designed to imitate a continental cathedral bell-tower, and which encases the standpipe, was not added until 1867. At its peak, the Kew Bridge Pumping Station delivered 30 million gallons of water a day to a wide area of west London. Steam power was replaced by diesel in 1934, and electric power in 1942. In 1986 the works went out of use when a new electric pumping station was built alongside it, and water is still pumped from there.

The museum features the world's largest collection of stationary water pumping engines.

Suffragettes

In 1913, two suffragettes were jailed for a protest in which they attacked one of the glasshouses at the Royal Botanic Gardens, Kew, and burned down the tea pavilion.

Syon House

Syon Abbey, established in Brentford in 1431 and destroyed by Henry VIII, is now the site of Syon House, London home of the Percy family, Dukes of Northumberland. The master mason to the Adams brothers, who built Syon House, was Thomas Hardwick, of a Brentford family that also built Somerset House and many London churches. Hardwick also tutored J. M. W. Turner and helped establish his career as an artist. Turner lived, as a child, above The Weir public house, then The White Horse.

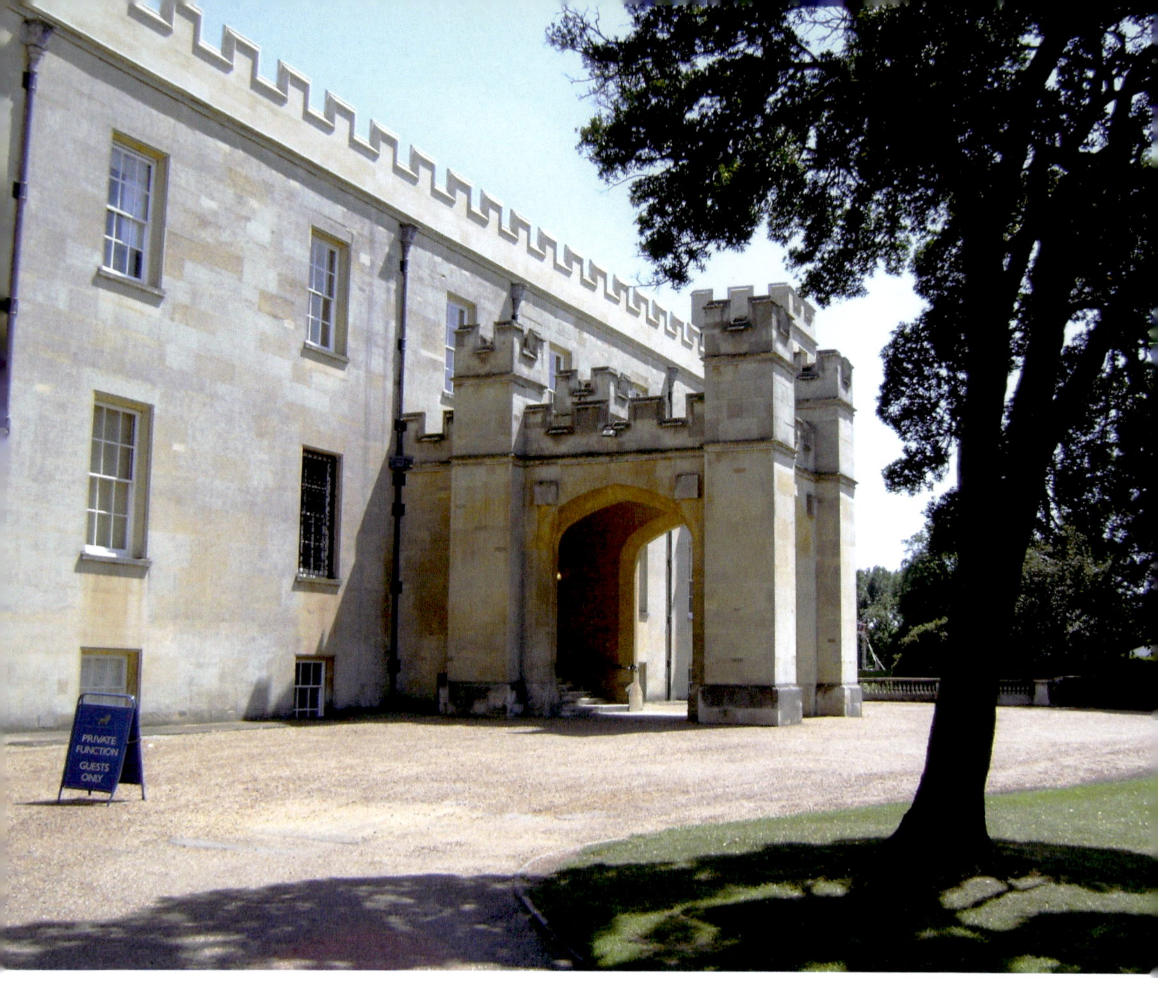

Above: Syon House, where Lady Jane Grey once lived. (Maxwell Hamilton and Kent Wang under Creative Commons)

Below: The Temperate House, Kew Gardens. (Daniel Case under Creative Commons)

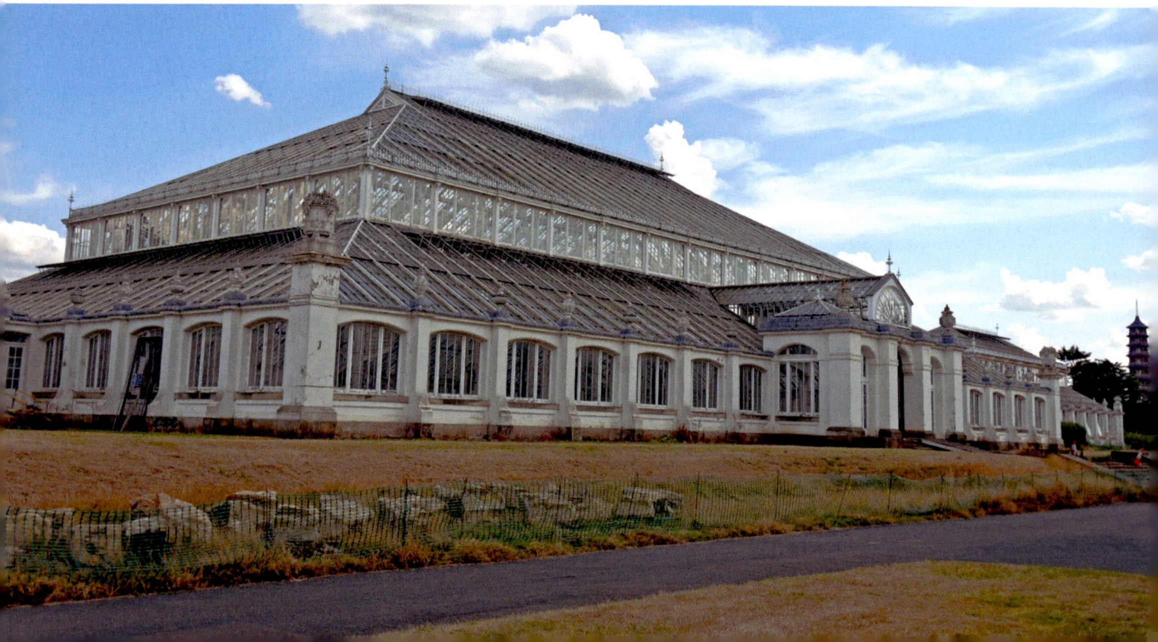

Temperate House

The Temperate House was the second great building to be erected in Kew Gardens, after the Palm House. It was opened in 1865, the brainchild of Sir William Hooker, the first director of the botanic gardens, and the designer Decimus Burton.

It was designed to showcase the splendour of the world's temperate zones, and today houses 10,000 individual plants from 1,500 species whose native homes are in Africa, Australia, New Zealand, the Americas, Asia and the Pacific Islands, many of them under threat.

The Temperate House was hugely experimental in its design at the time, an early exercise in combining a wrought-iron structure with walls of glass. It is beautifully detailed, with its rainwater drainpipes hidden in stone columns.

The lake beside it was created in order to make a virtue out of a necessity. So much gravel had to be extracted to form its terraces that a gaping hole was dug alongside it. Once landscaped, the lake provided became an attraction in itself.

By the start of the present century, the building was showing signs of decay. Rainwater was seeping into the iron, causing it to push against masonry, which then crumbled away. In 2011 an appeal was launched to raise the £15 million needed to restore it to its former glory.

Three Brentfords

There were once three Brentfords: until the latter part of the nineteenth century there were Old Brentford, New Brentford and Brentford End, each administered by a different authority (respectively Ealing, Hanwell and Isleworth). Then, in 1874, Old and New Brentford were amalgamated to form what is now known as Brentford. Brentford End remained a part of Isleworth.

Old Brentford was the area of town to the east, running from Gunnersbury Park in the north to the Thames at Kew Bridge in the south, and west to Boston Lane and Half Acre. New Brentford took in Boston Manor House and The Butts, with Brentford End running west from Brentford Bridge.

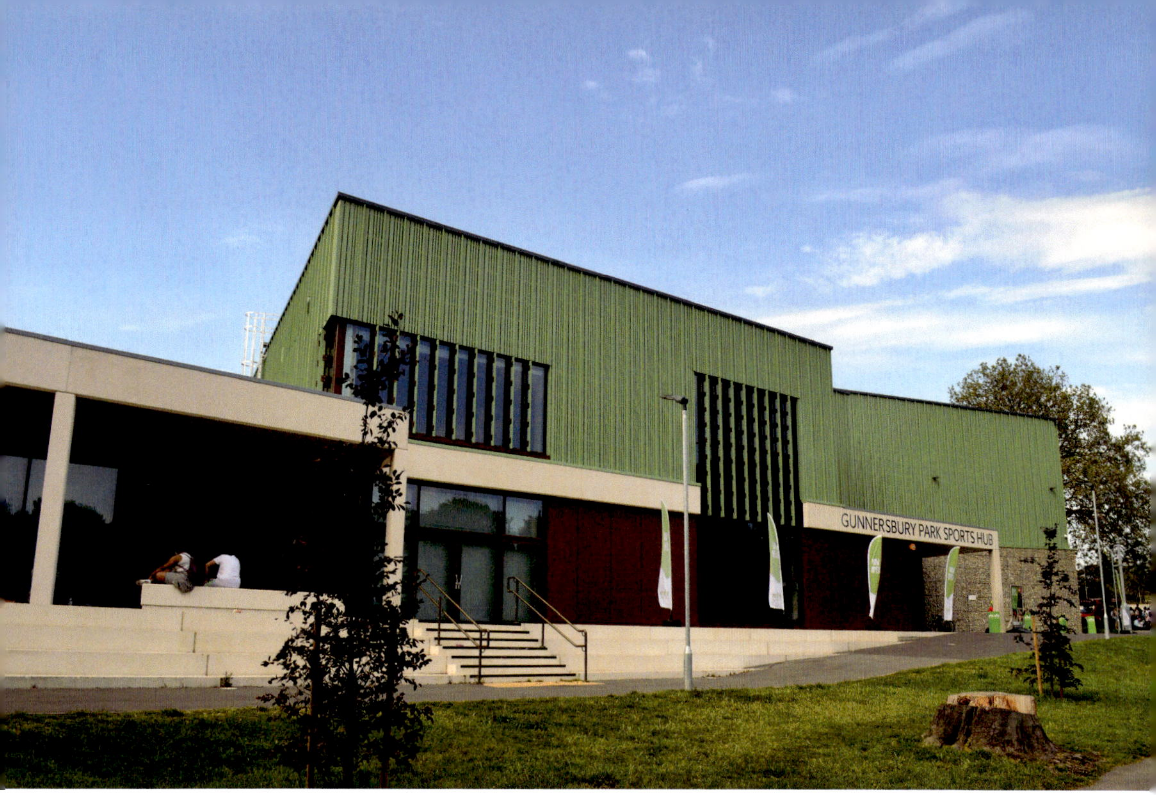

Above and below: Gunnersbury Park, once in old Brentford, and The Butts, once in New Brentford. (Andy Scott under Creative Commons)

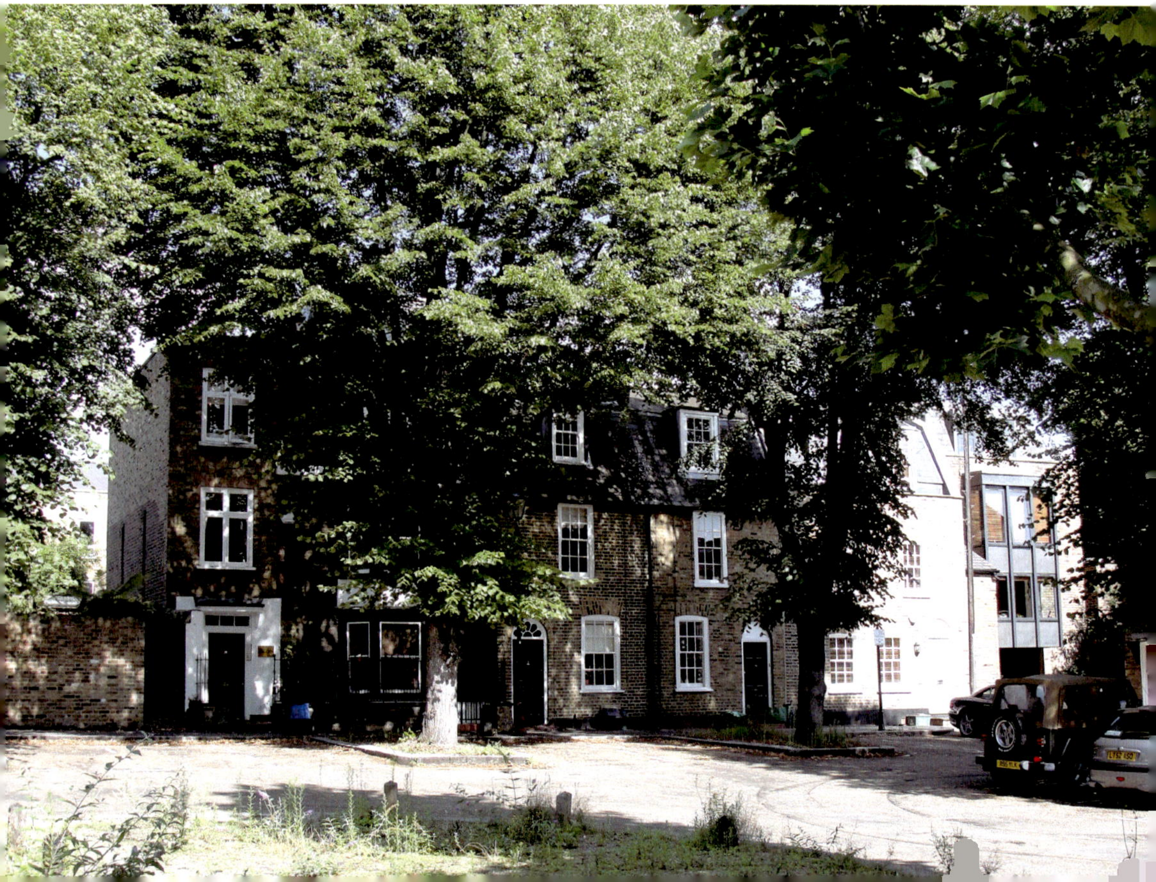

Old Brentford was divided into Upper Side and Lower Side, the former featuring the wide-open spaces of Gunnersbury, and the latter the far more rough and ready, densely populated riverside area around Brentford High Street and the wharves and docks along the Thames.

New Brentford was as geographically and socially distinct from Hanwell as Old Brentford was from Ealing.

Two Kings of Brentford

In 1671 George Villiers, Duke of Buckingham, featured characters called the two kings of Brentford in his play *The Rehearsal*. The play was a satire on contemporary dramas featuring what were effectively the super-heroes of the day: characters who spouted impossibly high-sounding moral sentiments and achieved seemingly unachievable goals. Buckingham has one of his characters explain:

> The chief hinge of this play, upon which the whole plot moves and turns … is, that I suppose two Kings to be of the same place: as, for example, at Brentford, for I love to write familiarly.
>
> Now the people having the same relations to 'em both, the same affections, the same duty, the same obedience, and all that; are divided among themselves in point of devoir [duty] and interest, how to behave themselves equally between 'em: these Kings differing sometimes in particular; though, in the main, they agree.

The Rehearsal was a huge hit, and the leading actors David Garrick and Colley Cibber both starred during long West End runs.

The play and its theme entered the popular consciousness and are referred to by a number of other writers. Robert Browning says of himself and another leading poet: 'Tennyson and I seem now to be regarded as the two kings of Brentford.' William Makepeace Thackeray wrote two poems on the topic of the two kings.

Buckingham's play was reworked by Sheridan for *The Critic* (1779), where the target of the satire is the pretentious prose of theatre critics. William Cowper's *The Task* includes the lines:

> United yet divided, twain at once:
> So sit two kings of Brentford on one throne.

U

Underwood and Son

Among the tangle of barge-builders, repair shops, saw mills, timber yards, maltings, corn and coal merchants crammed into the area between Brentford High Street and the River Brent was Underwood and Son, Hay and Straw Merchants.

Many of those businesses closed long ago, and the area is largely redeveloped, or in the process of development. Underwood's warehouse, which had been in business for 100 years, was knocked down in 2010 when the area it stood on, to the south of the High Street and alongside Dock Road, was cleared.

The boatyard on Lots Ait is one of the few remaining traditional businesses in Brentford. (Andy Scott under Creative Commons)

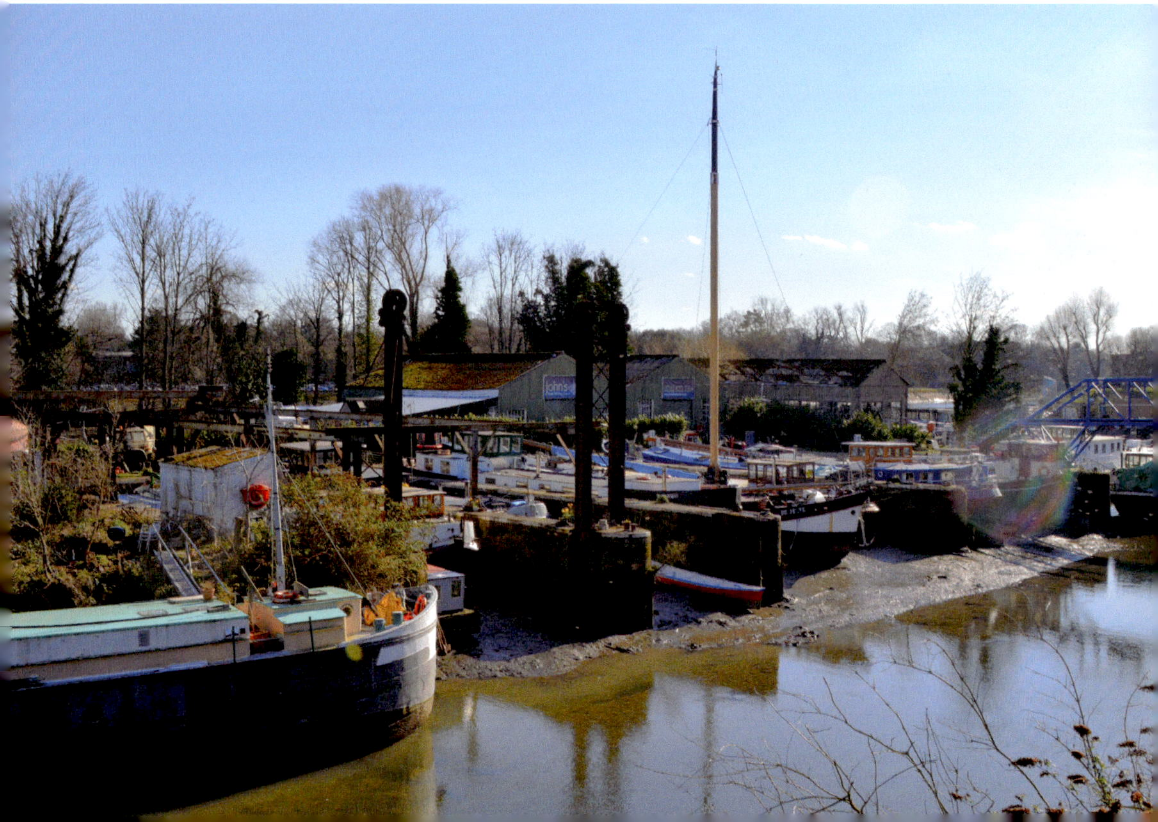

U

As the *Brentfordhistory* website relates, Edwin Underwood came to Brentford in 1865, to work as goods superintendent at Brentford Docks, overseeing the transfer of loads between river and railway. He had a highly successful career in what today would be called logistics, working previously in the West Country and the Midlands, developing great expertise in moving goods around the country.

Underwood clearly had entrepreneurial flair, and a desire to go into business on his own account. In 1871 he set up his hay and straw yard with his son, initially behind No. 80 High Street. Nine years later they had expanded, with offices at No. 79 High Street, and were living at No. 80. By 1894 they were also coal, coke and lime merchants, with premises at the railway yard then in Lionel Road, later adding a branch at Brentford Market, since replaced by the Fountain Leisure Centre.

Edwin Underwood became a pillar of the community, serving as both a magistrate and a councillor. By the early years of the last century, Underwood and Son had expanded internationally. As Janet McNamara writes in the *Brentford and Chiswick Local History Journal*:

> The company was an early importer of hay and straw, starting with 600 tons of forage per annum from Holland. This had increased to 100,000 tons early in the twentieth century. The Underwoods opened factories on the Continent for threshing and pressing and eventually had six depots in London and others in major cities around the country. The company employed 300 people and maintained a stable of 100 horses.

While the original warehouse has gone, No. 80 High Street survived the downturn in Brentford's fortunes that followed the Second World War, one of the few eighteenth-century houses in the town still standing. Janet McNamara writes: 'In 1951 it was listed as a building of architectural interest. The listing makes particular mention of the "Graceful porch with Tower of the Winds columns and pilasters and entablature with carved frieze".'

V1 and V2 Flying Bombs

The V1 was an early cruise missile developed by the Germans in the Second World War and designed to terrorise. It was known to its potential victims as a doodle bug or buzz bomb after the sound it made as it fell towards its target.

In August 1944, the children of Boston Manor House Infants School had to abandon their classrooms for three months when a V1 damaged the school and demolished two nearby houses. They went to St Paul's School, Brentford, until repairs could be completed.

Other V1s hit several targets in Brentford, one destroying a wood mill in Ferry Lane and damaging the gas works.

The V2 was even more terrifying: it flew at supersonic speed and was completely silent, giving no warning of its approach. This was the world's first long-range guided ballistic missile. One – only the second to hit London – fell on West Park Avenue, Kew, on 12 September 1944, destroying eight houses and causing extensive damage to the Chrysler factory which was assembling fuselages for war planes.

W

Watermans Arts Centre

One of the earliest schemes to reinvigorate Brentford's waterfront came in 1984 when the Watermans Arts Centre was opened on a site previously occupied, from 1820, by Brentford Gas Company.

The centre, with 239-seat theatre, 125-seat cinema, gallery, bar and restaurant, was first mooted in 1972, but raising the necessary funds proved to be a struggle. It opened with a concert by the sitar player Ravi Shankar. Robert Rankin, author of *The Brentford Trilogy*, held a writer's residency there in the 1980s.

The Watermans Arts Centre.

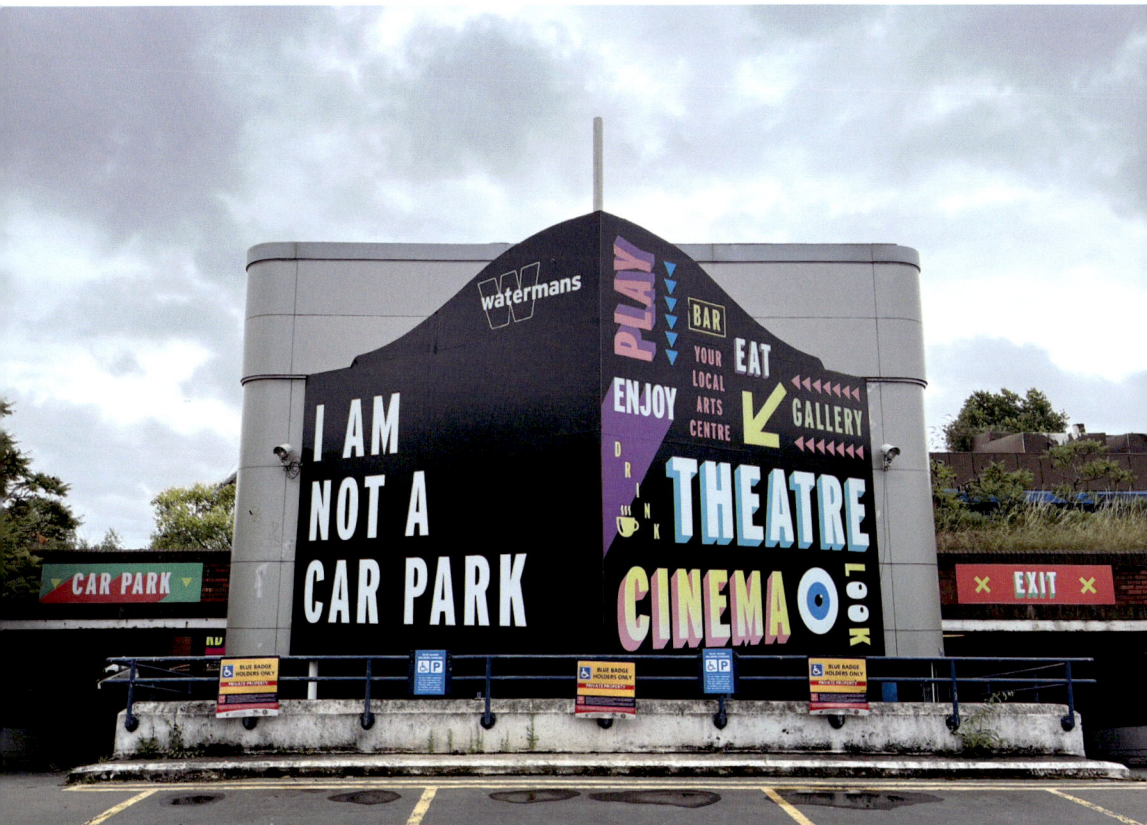

At the time of writing, plans were in the pipeline to redevelop the Watermans site for housing and relocate the arts centre to a new home on Half Acre, where Brentford's former police station stands, unoccupied.

Wholesale Fruit and Vegetable Market, Brentford

In the nineteenth and twentieth centuries, Brentford had a substantial purpose-build fruit and veg market, a sort of Covent Garden of west London, but it was started by accident.

In 1888 a market gardener from Cranford, 6 miles to the west, stopped his cart on the way to Covent Garden and went into the Express Tavern in Kew Bridge Road for a drink.

While he was there, someone asked to buy a bunch of his turnips. They must have been good, because when he stopped at the Express on his next trip to Covent Garden, several more people bought veg from him. Deciding that he could save himself the

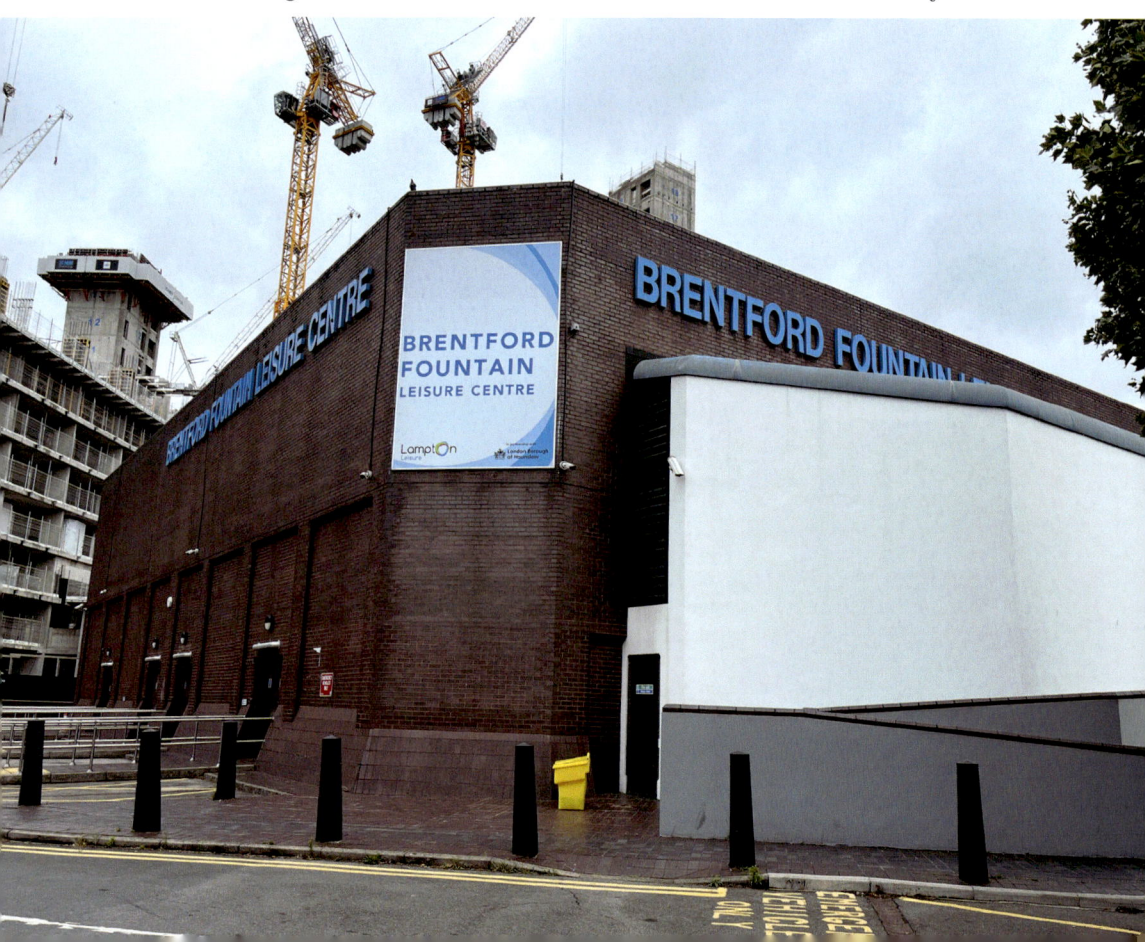

A market covering 11 acres once stood where the Fountain Leisure Centre is today.

long trek into central London, he got the landlord's permission to set up a stall outside the pub.

Soon, other market gardeners joined him, setting up around a fountain that stood in the centre of the road on the approach to the bridge. There was also a separate, long-established official market in Market Place, in the centre of Brentford.

This new market was unlicensed, but became so popular that, in the 1890s, up to sixty carts laden with produce were drawn up here, restricting the flow of traffic over the bridge. Such was the congestion that Brentford Local Board decided to find an official site and make money by charging the traders to sell there.

In 1893 the board bought 2.5 acres of land from Leopold de Rothschild on the fringe of his Gunnersbury Park estate. It was further north on Kew Bridge Road, where the Fountain Leisure Centre is now, and proved hugely popular, operating seven days a week. So much so that further land was bought and, in 1906, a covered market was established. A local newspaper, the *Middlesex Independent*, described it as 'the latest and most palatial market in Britain'. It was certainly substantial: fourteen shops lined the road at the front, a banana-ripening room was created and tropical fruit, unloaded from barges at Kew Bridge, was traded.

Further land was bought until, by 1921, the market occupied 11 acres, covering the whole of the north side of the road from the railway line up to what is now the Chiswick roundabout.

By the 1960s, when traders were using large lorries, the market buildings, designed for hand carts and horse-drawn wagons, were no longer suitable. A new site was found in Southall, and in 1974 the traders moved to the new Western International Market.

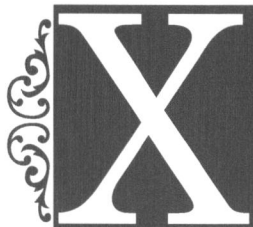

X Bee Inspired

X Bee Inspired is a part of the marketing and merchandising strategy of Brentford Football Club and echoes one of their slogans, which champion inclusion and acceptance of difference. Others include Bee Kind and Bee Together.

A range of clothing is marketed under the X Bee Inspired name. The Bee logo, which features prominently, comes from the club nickname, The Bees, but it got that name through a misunderstanding.

During the 1894–5 season, when Brentford's nickname was simply The Bs, a sports reporter misheard the crowd's chant of 'Buck Up, Bs', and after he included 'Buck Up, Bees' in his match report the name stuck.

Y

York Mineral Water Company

The great and the good enjoyed soft drinks produced by the York Mineral Water Company of York Road, Brentford. Its ginger beer, tonic water and other products were stamped 'By Special Appointment to His Majesty the King' and 'By appointment to the House of Lords'.

The firm, founded in 1896, closed in the 1960s.

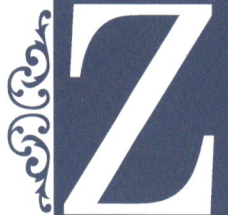

Zoffany, Johann

The Royal portrait painter Johann Zoffany (1733–1810) is buried at St Anne's Church on Kew Green. Zoffany, who was born in Germany, came to London in 1760 and was commissioned by George III to paint a number of royal portraits. He was appointed a member of the Royal Academy in 1769, and his work hangs in The National Gallery, Tate Britain, and The Royal Collection.

However, St Anne's chose to reject an altarpiece he created for the church. In it, local fishermen served as models for a depiction of The Last Supper. It was rejected by the church because Judas was modelled on a prominent church member, a lawyer who

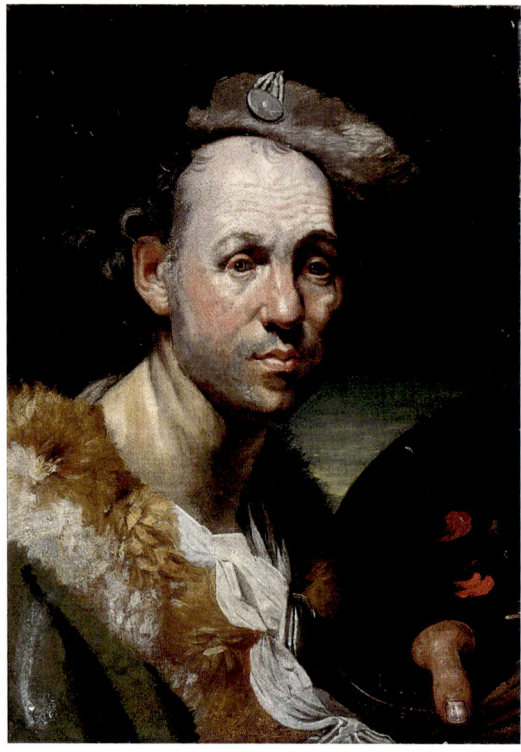

Johann Zoffany's *Portrait of an Unknown Artist*. (Christies)

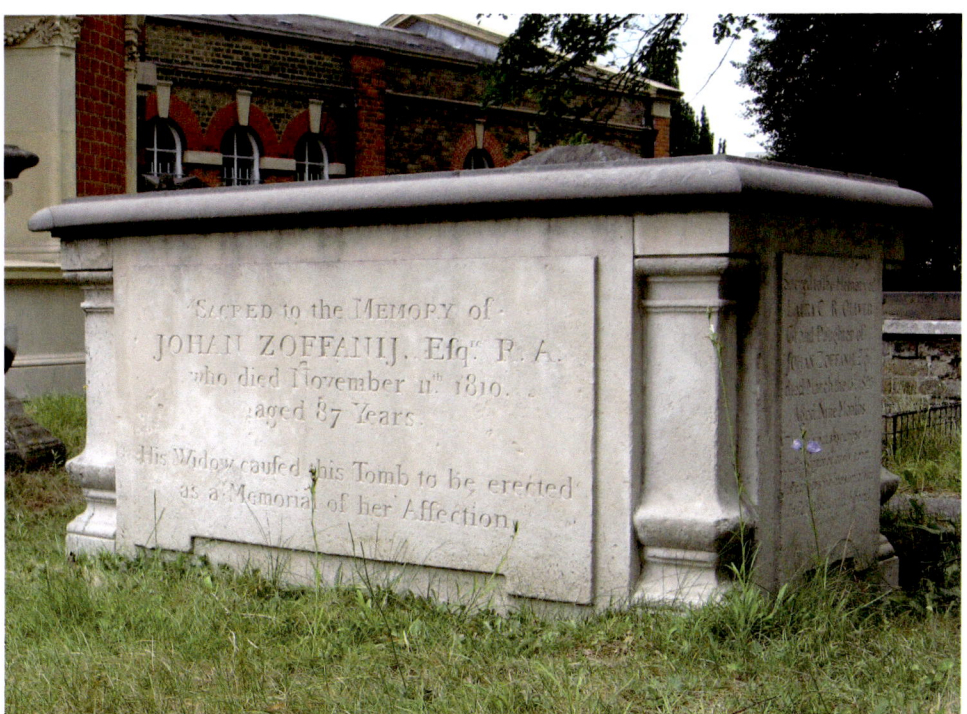

Zoffany's grave at St Anne's, Kew Green. (tpholland under Creative Commons)

Zoffany had fallen out with over making his will. Among the other figures, Zoffany appeared in the character of St Peter, with his wife as St John. St Anne's refused to pay for the altarpiece unless he repainted it. Zoffany refused and gave it to St George's Church, Brentford. It is now in another of the town's churches: St Paul's.

Zoffany was a colourful character. He had two wives, possibly marrying the second, who was only fourteen at the time, bigamously. He also had at least one other long-term partner plus other lovers.

While physically unprepossessing – described as being ugly and with a squint – he had great charm, a gift for friendship and an extravagant, flamboyant and generous nature.

He lived for the last twenty years of his life in Chiswick, at No. 65 Strand-on-the-Green, now known as Zoffany House.

Bibliography

Anonymous *The Beautiful History of Club Crests, Club Colours & Nicknames* https://thebeautifulhistory.wordpress.com/clubs/brentford/

Anonymous *The Life and Death of the Firestone Factory* https://www.modernism-in-metroland.co.uk/

Anonymous *Underwood's Hay and Straw Depot, Dock Road* https://brentfordhistory.com/

Anonymous, *Brentford High Street Project* http://www.bhsproject.co.uk/pubs_poem.shtml

Anonymous, *Lucozade Sign* https://brentfordhistory.com/2014/02/05/lucozade-sign/

Blomfield, David, *Kew Past* (Chichester: Phillimore, 1994)

Brentford History *Fifty Pubs of Brentford* https://brentfordhistory.com/2013/10/31/fifty-pubs-of-brentford/

Clegg, Gillian, *Brentford Past* (London: Historical Publications, 2002)

Cope, Nigel, *Brentfords buyer insists on a clean sheet* https://www.independent.co.uk/news/business/brentfords-buyer-insists-on-a-clean-sheet-1589944.html

Londonist *London Made Motors* https://londonist.com/2015/11/london-made-motors

Longhurst, Chris *10 things you might not know about Brentford's Golden Mile* https://www.mylondon.news/news/west-london-news/10-things-you-might-not-7948068

McNamara, Janet *An American Ambassador's View of Brentford* https://brentfordandchiswicklhs.org.uk/an-american-ambassadors-view-of-brentford-in-1815/

McNamara, Janet *Beach's Of Brentford: The World Famous Jam* https://brentfordandchiswicklhs.org.uk/

McNamara, Janet *Number 80 Brentford High Street* (Brentford & Chiswick Local History Journal 12, 2003)

Nicholl, Charles, *The Lodger: Shakespeare on Silver Street* (London: Penguin, 2008)

Roberts, Cecil, *And So to Bath* (London: Hodder and Stoughton, 1940)

Sharman, Helen, *Thoughts from Space* https://kewtw9.org/event/thoughts-from-space/

Turner, William, *A new herball, wherin are conteyned the names of herbes* (London: Mierdman, 1551)